Women with Adult ADHD

An Unconventional Guide to Breaking Through Barriers! Learn Essential Life Skills from Theory to Practice to Deal with ADHD and Stop Feeling Like a Failure

Rose Hoskins

© **Copyright 2022 - All rights reserved.**

The content contained within this book may not be reproduced, duplicated or transmitted without direct written permission from the author or the publisher.

Under no circumstances will any blame or legal responsibility be held against the publisher, or author, for any damages, reparation, or monetary loss due to the information contained within this book. Either directly or indirectly.

Legal Notice:

This book is copyright protected. This book is only for personal use. You cannot amend, distribute, sell, use, quote or paraphrase any part, or the content within this book, without the consent of the author or publisher.

Disclaimer Notice:

Please note the information contained within this document is for educational and entertainment purposes only. All effort has been executed to present accurate, up to date, and reliable, complete information. No warranties of any kind are declared or implied. Readers acknowledge that the author is not engaging in the rendering of legal, financial, medical or professional advice. The content within this book has been derived from various sources. Please consult a licensed professional before attempting any techniques outlined in this book.

By reading this document, the reader agrees that under no circumstances is the author responsible for any losses, direct or indirect, which are incurred as a result of the use of information contained within this document, including, **but not limited to, — errors, omissions, or inaccuracies.**

TABLE OF CONTENTS:

Women with Adult ADHD _____ 1

Introduction _____ 8

Part one- ADHD: what it is, symptoms in women and diagnosis 12

Chapter 1: ADHD in Brief _____ 12

What is ADHD? _____ 12

How does ADHD come about? _____ 15

ADHD in adults and women _____ 16

The various types of ADHD _____ 17

Chapter 2: Causes and Symptoms of ADHD _____ 20

The causes of ADHD _____ 20

Risk factors for ADHD _____ 21

Symptoms of ADHD_____ 23

Symptoms in the child: inattention and hyperactivity _____ 24

Symptoms in adults_____ 26

Symptoms in the adult woman _____ 27

Chapter 3: the correct diagnosis in women with ADHD _____ 31

The diagnosis of ADHD in adults_____ 31

The Self-Assessment for a Diagnosis of ADHD _____ 33

Diagnosis in female ADHD _____ 34

Part Two- Overview of Effective Therapies for ADHD _____ 35

Chapter 4: Therapies for ADHD. A little background for the adult woman_____ 35

What to do if you are diagnosed with ADHD? ... 35
Diagnosis of ADHD in adult women: what you need to know ... 37
Chapter 5: Pharmacological therapies for the child with ADHD. 39
A little background: one-on-one, multimodal treatment for ADHD ... 39
Drug therapy ... 40
Conclusions on drug therapy ... 45
Chapter 6: Psycho-Behavioral Therapy for the Child with ADHD. ... 47
Psycho-behavioral treatment ... 47
Behavioral therapy or counseling ... 47
Parent training ... 49
School-based interventions for the child with ADHD: Teacher Training ... 53
Intervention with the child ... 55
Conclusions on psycho-behavioral therapy ... 57
Chapter 7: The Effective Therapies for the Woman with ADHD. 59
A multimodal approach also for the adult woman with ADHD ... 59
Drug therapy in women with ADHD ... 60
Alternative to drugs: Homeopathy and Phytotherapy ... 62
Psychoeducation for the adult woman with ADHD ... 65
Psychosocial treatment in the adult woman with ADHD ... 66
Alternative approaches for adult women with ADHD ... 68
Other interventions for the adult woman with ADHD ... 71
Alternative tools for the adult with ADHD. ... 74
Conclusions on therapies for the adult woman with ADHD ... 75

Part three- how to manage emotions in women with ADHD __ 77

Chapter 8: Emotional dysregulation for the adult woman with ADHD. _____ 77

Moods and emotions for the adult woman with ADHD _____ 77

Emotional dysregulation in those with ADHD _____ 78

What are the typical characteristics of emotional dysregulation ____ 80

Chapter 9: Emotion management for the woman with ADHD. 82

What anxiety disorder in women with ADHD consists of _____ 82

How to combat anxiety disorder if you have ADHD _____ 83

Some tips to be able to manage anxiety at the best _____ 85

Practical tips on how to manage emotions _____ 86

Part four: proper nutrition and lifestyle to be able to manage ADHD _____ 93

Chapter 10: Ideal Nutrition for a Woman with ADHD _____ 93

The importance of a healthy and proper diet in those with ADHD___ 93

What is and what is the specific diet for those suffering from ADHD 96

How to create a personalized ADHD diet_____ 97

The best supplements and vitamins for those with ADHD _____ 99

Chapter 11: Sports Activity for Women with ADHD._____ 105

How exercise helps counteract ADHD symptoms _____ 105

The best exercises for children and adolescents suffering from ADHD _____ 106

The best exercises for adult women with ADHD _____ 107

Part Five: Managing ADHD from a purely mental perspective 109

Chapter 12: The Importance of Meditation_____ 109

Application of Mindfulness in ADHD _____ 110

The Transcendental Meditation method to combat ADHD _____ 112

How yoga can help combat ADHD _____ 114

What are the benefits of meditative methods in those with ADHD _ 116

Part Six: How to manage relationships if you have ADHD _____ 118

Chapter 13: Relationship Management for the Woman with ADHD. _____ 118

Relational problems associated with ADHD _____ 118

Helpful tips on how to improve your romantic relationship with your partner if you have ADHD _____ 119

How to improve the sexual sphere if you suffer from ADHD _____ 123

How to overcome difficulties in the sexual arena if you have ADHD 124

How to raise and manage your children if you have ADHD _____ 126

Part Seven: How to manage work and money for the woman with ADHD _____ 130

Chapter 14: Work issues for the woman with ADHD. _____ 130

Women, work and ADHD: some statistics _____ 130

Practical tips on how to get and keep a job _____ 131

Chapter 15: Money Management for the Woman with ADHD 134

Tips on how to manage money _____ 134

Part Eight - Time Management Tips _____ 137

Chapter 16: Some useful and practical techniques for having a good general demeanor with ADHD _____ 137

20 Tips for Good Behavior for the Adult Woman with ADHD _____ 137

Chapter 17: Mini-guide on how to manage time effectively __ 147

How does ADHD affect poor time management? 147

Understanding the difficulties of time management with ADHD 148

Best tips for time management 148

The Grossman Model 152

Conclusions 155

Introduction

This second manual, along with the first one, was developed and written with the purpose of bringing the public aware of ADHD (i.e., the disorder known by the acronym Attention Deficit/Hyperactivity Disorder). In this second manual, in a particular way, the disorder will be treated from a purely practical point of view, in anticipation of the fact that this pathology has been diagnosed in an adult woman. This is because, although it is a pathology that is usually recognized in childhood, it may happen that it is not diagnosed and treated at this stage of life.

For this purpose, therefore, was born the main idea of this manual: this, in fact, will be a practical guide aimed at women who suffer from this disorder diagnosed in adulthood.

But why a guide aimed specifically at women with ADHD? For a number of main reasons, one of which has to do with the fact that, for many women, life with ADHD must not have been at all easy, and it's time to be aware that this disorder can bring serious difficulties that, from the past, can still have repercussions in everyday life.

This is in turn because, as we mentioned in the first manual and as will be briefly taken up in this one, attention deficit hyperactivity disorder affects the way a woman might turn her attention to others or in her daily activities, stay still and focused but, more importantly, it could result in a lack of control in behavior, leading to far more serious consequences.

The main purpose, therefore, of this second guide is not only to raise awareness among adult women about the
problem of ADHD and to no longer neglect it, increasing not only your knowledge but also your positive interest in this disorder. It is only right, in fact, as we did in the first manual, to make you aware of all the possible implications that the disease can have both for you as an adult woman and for your family, in the school, work, social, relational and even professional spheres.

Although this disorder has certainly made your life much more complicated than it should be, however, you will be able to discover for yourself, thanks to this guide, that this is a condition that is not only medically treatable but also perfectly manageable in your daily life. And so, in this way you will be able to see all the implications in a positive sense.

Starting with the fact that it is only fair that you know that, as far as ADHD is concerned, you are not alone, and that it is not an unknown, incurable and rare condition. Just think of the statistics that see, especially in the United States, attention deficit disorder (ADHD) in constant increase. According to statistics, in fact, it is assumed that in the United States affects more than one in ten children between the ages of 5 and 17 years out of nearly 200 thousand children analyzed. But despite the continued interest and increasing research regarding ADHD, the most troubling thing about the occurrence of this behavior disorder is that it continues to go unrecognized and therefore untreated in childhood. For this reason, many women find themselves discovering as adults that the cause of likely poor performance in school, may be related to the very presence of this disorder. As we said above, the increasing occurrence in adulthood, especially for women, is related to the fact that this disorder is often not recognized as a child and therefore continues into adulthood with consequences that are often not so easy to manage. The most important thing for you, of course, if you have received a definite diagnosis of ADHD, is that this should represent neither the end of the world nor the end of your social relationships or your possible professional or personal success. If in the first manual we took care to unite and incorporate all the theoretical aspects as well as some practical ones of this pathology, in this second manual we will increase the practical knowledge. We will also provide you with advice on strategies to improve your situation, and consequently, your quality of life.

In the first book, therefore, we talked about the disease mainly on a theoretical level. If you have come to this second reading, you have already understood and recognized all there is to know about this pathology, its history and evolution, how it was born and what are the symptoms to recognize. Also in the first manual, there were some "practical" life hints where you were told all the right steps and actions to follow in case you were diagnosed with this type of pathology. And in this regard, there was extensive discussion on how to make a correct diagnosis of ADHD. You also already know what impact this type of disorder can have on your overall life, couple and family. It was also about discussing all the risks associated with this disorder and what impacts it can also have on the brain, with plenty of studies reported to support this theory. So not only on a theoretical level, but also on a practical one, we have come to your aid precisely to bring you up to speed on all the symptoms, and implications but also some possible solutions to deal with a path as a woman with ADHD. Speaking of solutions, these will be taken up and explored in this second part of the guide. In fact, you will be shown, specifically, what are all the possible practical strategies and all the treatments to alleviate the symptoms of this disease. These strategies will also be complemented by tips for managing your daily life.

Anyway, this second text will be structured as follows:

- ✓ The first part in which the main notions about ADHD will be resumed: that is, what is the disease, the main symptoms, the implications in daily life and how to make a possible diagnosis.
- ✓ A second part Overview of effective therapies for ADHD.
- ✓ The third part of which will pick up and address in even greater depth the intense emotions that this disorder can bring. But above all, we will talk about how to control them, through practical tips, combined with the control of emotions, and you will be shown healthy habits to adopt to manage ADHD. The second part will close with a vademecum on how to manage especially the anxiety associated with this disorder.
- ✓ A fourth part, even more practical, will delve into the discourse on nutrition and correct lifestyles to manage ADHD. Guidance will be given, therefore, on how to eat and what are the correct eating habits for those with ADHD. In addition to healthy eating, there will be guidance on sleep habits and how sports can help.
- ✓ The fifth part of the text, on the other hand, will look at the management of the pathology from a purely mental point of view: in fact, it will talk about effective daily routines, Mindfulness and meditations useful for ADHD and other

relaxation techniques such as those typical of Yoga to help you manage even the most negative emotions.
- ✓ The sixth part of the text, then, will be very important because it will deal with the management of emotional relationships for women with ADHD. From the sexual sphere to the family sphere, you will be shown how to manage your social life and above all make you understand that, despite the presence of such a socially compromising pathology, it is possible for you to have a healthy and full relational life.
- ✓ The seventh part of the manual, however, will be an economic part, which is purely about work and how to manage work relationships and your work with this disease but also a guide on how to manage money. You will therefore find tips on how to manage money and savings.
- ✓ In the eighth and final part of the manual, finally, 20 useful and practical techniques will be indicated to have a good general conduct with ADHD, but above all a mini-guide on how to manage time effectively, despite the presence of this pathology.

At the end of this second manual, therefore, you will understand that there are a whole series of therapies, strategies and habits that will make the disease completely manageable and lead you to have a normal life. As we indicated in the introduction of the first text, the main theme is and remains the thread that binds the reading path, which is precisely that of "accepting yourself exactly as you are. But in addition to accepting yourself, you also have the real possibility to improve your life, assuming that you are not irredeemable or antisocial. You will simply have to work a little harder than necessary to have a healthy life, made of real and concrete affection and friendships, as well as to realize yourself in the professional field. We recommend that you continue reading this second book to help you understand that you don't have to feel ashamed of being affected by ADHD, but that it is possible to live with this disorder and remain, extraordinary person, just as you are.

Part one- ADHD: what it is, symptoms in women and diagnosis

In this first part of the text, as already mentioned in the introduction, the main notions about ADHD will be taken up: what specifically is this pathology, the main symptoms, the implications in daily life, and how to make a possible diagnosis.

Chapter 1: ADHD in Brief

What is ADHD?

In this first chapter, we will briefly pick up and refresh your memory regarding the ADHD sketch. ADHD (whose acronym stands for Attention-Deficit/Hyperactivity Disorder) is the term in which a whole range of typical symptoms are identified. All of the symptoms associated with this term are dictated by behaviors that are considered dysfunctional, that is, behaviors that do not match one's tasks or goals. These dysfunctional behaviors are usually associated with states of inattention, impulsivity, and motor hyperactivity. This pattern of behavior is quite typical in children, but it also has strong repercussions in adulthood. This is one of the most important concepts, especially in view of the fact that this manual is aimed at women who have discovered they have ADHD. However, it is only fair to emphasize and reiterate to you that ADHD is not a disorder that occurs in adulthood, but is always linked to childhood. Therefore, even if you discovered it late in life, ADHD has always been with you throughout your life.

But, starting right from the infantile age, attention-deficit/hyperactivity disorder is, therefore, a scenario in which is perennially present a rather poor or almost completely absent duration of attention on the part of the child (and then in the adult, even in the woman). But inattention is often combined with a rather lively and excessively impulsive behavior. Now it is also necessary to remind you that these characteristics are not really appropriate to the age of the child, interfering also with its functionality or its own development. Imagine at this point that, even in adults who cannot sit still or complete a given task, ADHD continues to negatively affect the lives of those who suffer from it.

In addition to being a disorder that primarily affects a child's neurological development, ADHD is much more common than you might think. And not just in children, but in adults as well.

Attention-deficit/hyperactivity disorder (ADHD), in fact, can affect all age groups: according to recent statistics from the U.S., it affects about 5% of children of all ages.

Another very important thing to remember is that attention-deficit/hyperactivity disorder is a neuro-evolutionary disorder. To make this concept even clearer for you, the fact that it is a neuro-evolutionary disorder simply means that despite the hyperactive and impulsive behaviors and their dysfunctionality and inappropriateness in various contexts, ADHD is not part of behavioral disorders, such as antisocial behavior.

Thus, it is fair to say that ADHD is a developmental disorder that is associated with neurodevelopmental disorders. Specifically, neurodevelopmental disorders are conditions with a neurological correlation that may interfere with the acquisition, retention, or application of specific skills or sets of information. Included with these disorders are dysfunctions in attention, memory, perception, language, problem-solving skills, or social interaction. In other words, a person with ADHD is not a sociopathic individual. So, on a practical level, you need to get it out of your mind that you are someone who is socially irredeemable, or needs to be admitted to psychiatry.

So, the first thing you should definitely not do, in case you have been diagnosed with this condition is that you or your child may suffer from some mental disorder, or be considered dangerous people who could harm others.

The thorniest issue of ADHD always remains the process of diagnosing the pathology. Usually, it is diagnosed for the first time during childhood: but this is not always the case, on the contrary, as we have already seen in the first manual, often, the adult woman, in particular, recognizes the disease without knowledge of the cause, as for example when she discovers it in her own child. And what makes the situation worse is precisely the lack of a 100% certain diagnosis. As we have already noted in the first manual, in fact, there are many controversies related to the fact that this type of pathology is not always easy to diagnose. In any case, it is estimated that ADHD affects 8-11% of children of school age, with an incidence twice as high in males as in females (although the incidence of diagnosis seems to be subsequently higher in adult females, precisely because of the lack of diagnosis of the disease). Returning to the typical character aspects of this disorder for children is that this whole series of behaviors can significantly affect school performance and social relationships well into adulthood.

Children with attention deficit hyperactivity disorder, as well as adults, share common characteristics. These dysfunctional behaviors (hyperactivity, impulsivity, and inattention) or common characteristics, are nothing more than a direct result of the inability of the person with ADHD to have control over his or her responses to stimuli that come from the external environment. In addition to having this lack of attention and the feeling of being unable to perform any activity that requires its presence, the dysfunctional behavior also leads the subject with ADHD to have little ability to focus their attention on a single specific task.

All of these, we reiterate, is dysfunctional behaviors. Recognizing them and incorporating them as ADHD, however, is certainly not a simple matter. This is because, in addition to the diagnosis, even the symptomatic picture itself with all these dysfunctional behaviors, is the subject of much controversy, both for its dubious scientific basis, both for the use that is made by common sense. In summary, then, Attention Deficit/Hyperactivity Disorder is a typical childhood disorder of neurobiological origin and neuro-evolutionary type. Despite the growing interest and discoveries that are made every day on this disorder, it is still very complex to define in full with a symptomatology and a diagnosis certain. It must also be said that many adults, especially women, may never have a certain diagnosis of this disease, or even ignore its very existence. Geographically, too, this disease is not recognized everywhere: only in the United States is it fully treated, while in other parts of the world it is practically unknown. In fact, ADHD is still one of the most diagnosed childhood psychiatric disorders in Anglo-Saxon countries. In other areas of the world, however, it is not fully recognized in clinical practice. For this reason, and because it is still rather unknown, in many countries children do not receive adequate care for ADHD, experiencing quite a few difficulties in socialization and in the school environment. And often adults, and women, in particular, find themselves having to deal with symptoms and a pathology they have never heard of.

How does ADHD come about?

After reviewing the meaning of ADHD, we briefly show you the historical origins of this disorder. Historically, ADHD takes its cue from and replaces the so-called "hyperactive child syndrome", known first as "minimal brain damage" (until the late 60s), then as "minimal brain disorder" (presented in the DSM III, 1984). The name changed to ADHD precisely because there was no longer any reason for any explicit reference to brain damage or dysfunction.

Some authors (such as Carey W.B) believe that the new name has not in fact changed the mindset of those who use it, the assumption of brain damage remaining implicit.

But it is mainly thanks to the studies and work of Virginia Douglas (1972, 1979) that we have the real birth of the pathology as it is known today. The watershed comes from the fact that it emphasized the centrality of cognitive deficits compared to motor deficits, framed as an accessory factor with respect to the former.

Two subtypes of DDA were described in the DSM-III (APA, 1980): one with and one without Hyperactivity. There were 16 expected symptoms, divided into three categories:
- Inattention (5 symptoms)
- Impulsivity (6 symptoms)
- Hyperactivity (5 symptoms).

According to these criteria, the subject, to be diagnosed with DDA, had to present at least three symptoms of inattention and three of impulsivity; while if DDA was associated with Hyperactivity then at least 2 other symptoms should have been present.

Following the publication of the third revised edition of the DSM (DSM-III-R, 1987), Attention Deficit/Hyperactivity Disorder received recognition as the most studied childhood syndrome in the world. As a result of these discoveries, ADHD is now recognized, diagnosed, and treated disorder.

ADHD in adults and women

ADHD, we now know, is a typical childhood disorder. This is not to say, however, that there is no recognition in adults. On the contrary: ADHD is a mental disorder more commonly diagnosed in women in adulthood than we can imagine. As we have already reiterated to you, it is precisely for this reason that we decided to elaborate this text, to help women unaware even of the very existence of this disorder but to whom, later, it was diagnosed. Also, the fact that many do not know they have this type of disorder but experience all its negative aspects on a daily basis is more common than you might think.

At the statistical level, in fact, several studies have been carried out by the Observatories for Women's Health that deal with the main pathologies and issues of women's health on a daily basis (as well as promoting a culture of gender health). These studies have also been able to address the issues related to the incidence that this disorder continues to have in women: it is estimated that the diagnosis and incidence of this disease have seen, in the last year alone, an increase of 2%. But what happens when the disorder is not diagnosed as a child and continues into adulthood? On a neurological level, pretty much the same thing: the neurological differences that children with AHDH have to continue into adulthood, and, about half of the subjects, continue to present the behavioral symptoms typical of children with ADHD. With this, it is therefore possible to infer that the terminology and symptoms, conditions, and manifestations remain nearly the same. Adult ADHD (for both men and women) is therefore a mental health disorder that includes a combination of persistent and preexisting problems, such as difficulty paying attention for long periods of time, hyperactivity, and impulsive and sometimes inappropriate behavior. Although the terminology and symptoms appear to be almost the same, there is a slight difference. The difference can be found precisely in the symptomatology: all ADHD symptoms in adults, in fact, may not be as clearly manifested as ADHD symptoms in children. To give some practical examples, in adults, hyperactivity may decrease, but struggles with impulsivity, a perpetual state of restlessness, and difficulty paying attention or completing certain tasks may continue.

The main difference also lies in the diagnosis of ADHD itself: in fact, it can be much more difficult to detect in adulthood. The main reason for this difficulty in diagnosis, as we have often explained in the first manual, is that the symptoms of ADHD, are often confused with those of a typical mental disorder, such as disorders associated with anxiety or mood or obsessive-compulsive disorders.

The crucial issue for adults, therefore, remains diagnosis: in order to diagnose ADHD in adults, in fact, physicians must not only fully understand the problem through specific questionnaires, but they must also investigate the school history of the adult with possible ADHD: in fact, they may require to consult school records to confirm frequent episodes of inattention or impulsivity, even since then.

The various types of ADHD

Having explained how ADHD works for the adult subject, it is important to reiterate the concept that there is not just one type of ADHD. Precisely because of the fact that it is a disorder characterized by various dysfunctional behaviors, with as many varied symptoms, multiple types (or subtypes) have been identified to be traced back to the disorder.

ADHD can, in fact, be divided into 3 forms or subtypes:

1. In the so-called classic form, of which the major symptoms are hyperactivity, impulsivity and general attention disorder.
2. A less frequent and more difficult-to-recognize form in which only attention deficit appears (present mainly in females).
3. A third, is characterized by prevalent hyperactivity and impulsivity.

There is a further distinction in which they differ:
Inattention (ADHD with reduced attention).
Hyperactivity/impulsivity (ADHD with impulsivity and hyperactivity).
A combination of the two forms (combined ADHD, with inattention and impulsivity/hyperactivity).

With the first subtype, namely the inattentive one, the ADHD disorder will manifest itself as one who experiences general and ongoing difficulties in sustaining attention, following a speech, and organizing his activities or completing them. In addition to being inattentive, he always tries to avoid or show disappointment in engaging in tasks that require sustained mental effort over time. In practice, in addition to lacking the capacity of focal attention, i.e. focusing on something, the inattentive subtype lacks the capacity of "sustained" attention. This means that this subtype lacks the ability to maintain sustained attention over time during school, work, or simple daily activities. Without this sustained capacity, the subject with ADHD is very easily distracted and will tend to lose the tools of the trade, with unpleasant repercussions on his intellectual performance.

As for the second subtype, the hyperactive-impulsive one, it must be said that it is the most difficult to recognize. This subtype, in fact, is diagnosed much more rarely than the other two clinical forms. In any case, this subtype has typical difficulties in playing or engaging in quiet activities and is unable to sit or stay still. The hyperactive-impulsive subtype, in practice, represents the restlessness of made person. If we analyze instead, the impulsive component of the subtype, it is necessary to reiterate that it mainly concerns the inability to procrastinate in time the response to an external or internal stimulus.

Finally, the third subtype, the combined subtype, has both problem areas. In essence, the third subtype represents a combination of these two specific problem areas. After going over the complete ADHD sketch, in the next chapter, we will briefly show you what the causes and symptoms of this disorder are.

Chapter 2: Causes and Symptoms of ADHD

The causes of ADHD

In this chapter we will go over what causes and symptoms of ADHD. It is only fair to reiterate, as we did in the first manual, that a certain and univocal cause of ADHD does not exist, but several competing causes are hypothesized. In fact, research is still ongoing, so many of the causes and risk factors for ADHD are still almost completely unknown. Despite the general uncertainty, the current research nevertheless shows a rather dominant factor represented by genetics that plays, in any case, a really key role in many pathologies. In this case, it is assumed also of ADHD.

However, in spite of the progress made, it is only possible, in fact, to hypothesize in theory that a multiplicity of factors may contribute to the origin of this pathology, the most likely of which are those purely related to the genetic component as primary, while those related to the social and physical conditions of the child as secondary.

Thus, genetic or hereditary factors, represent, in 75% of cases, the main cause of ADHD disorder. The onset of ADHD disorder can therefore be considered hereditary or related to the brain morphology of the subject who suffers from it. But it can also depend on prenatal, perinatal or traumatic factors. Of course, these are always hypothetical factors that are still subject to several demonstrative studies.

The research then determined that ADHD is probably caused by other factors, again hypothetical related to pregnancy and the very early years of life, such as:

- ✓ Alterations in neurotransmitters in general during fetal formation (substances that transmit nerve impulses to the brain).
- ✓ Some environmental factors, such as exposure during pregnancy and during the very first years of life to alcohol and

smoking (it is known, in fact, that nicotine may cause hypoxia, i.e. lack of oxygen in the fetus).
- ✓ Probable lead exposure during pregnancy can also be a major risk factor.
- ✓ Complications during pregnancy and childbirth.
- ✓ Premature birth may be a risk factor.
- ✓ Infectious infections and diseases, such as chickenpox, are also contracted during pregnancy, at birth, or in the early years of life.
- ✓ Some other risk factors are low birth weight (less than 1500 grams).

Other risk factors, are purely related to deficits, or alterations in the central nervous system.
These alterations then have direct consequences especially with regard to some functions performed by specific areas of the brain. Specific areas that regulate attention and the ability to concentrate. These deficits can also be caused by head injuries, brain infections, iron deficiency, obstructive sleep apnea, and exposure to lead, as well as alcohol, tobacco, or cocaine, before birth.
In conclusion, attention deficit hyperactivity disorder does not recognize a single specific cause of origin. In fact, the onset of this disorder seems to depend on the interaction of various environmental, social, behavioral, biochemical, and genetic factors.

Risk factors for ADHD

In the previous paragraph, we discussed the possible and hypothetical causes of ADHD. To be even more correct, when we talk about ADHD, in fact, we refer more to the risk factors, rather than to the actual causes. In any case, there are correlations (or risk factors) for which this pathology may arise within a subject. In addition to occurring, these factors contribute directly to the increase of the disease itself. And this translates into greater risk factors that correspond to greater episodes of onset of the disease. At this point, we will briefly list the risk factors for ADHD are:

- The first risk factor corresponds to genetics and familiarity (parents, siblings) with ADHD or other mental disorders.
- A second was related to maternal misbehavior such as alcoholism, smoking, and drug use during pregnancy.
- A third risk factor involves exposure to environmental toxins in childhood such as lead traced primarily in dyes or pipes from old buildings.
- Premature birth and complications during childbirth may also be other risk factors for the onset of ADHD.
- Another factor, still being studied, is iron deficiency.

Regarding the first factor examined, namely the genetic/familial factor, several studies have been able to show that there are many genes implicated in the etiology of ADHD including various polymorphisms of genes that regulate the dopaminergic system.

In addition to the risk factors that are purely inherent in the ADHD subject, there are also external risk factors, or as we defined them better, environmental risk factors. Environmental risk factors include and are recognized as all those behaviors that are incorrect on the part of the mother of the future unborn child, such as cigarette smoking and the use of alcohol during pregnancy. These behaviors are absolute to be avoided not only to prevent a possible ADHD but many other negative consequences on the health and development of the fetus during pregnancy.

Other environmental risk factors include pre-pregnancy maternal overweight or obesity states, preeclampsia, hypertension, Paracetamol exposure, and smoking during pregnancy. In addition, certain childhood atopic diseases have been strongly associated with ADHD.

Previous family studies have indicated that maternal pre-pregnancy obesity, overweight, and smoking during pregnancy are confounded by familial or genetic factors, and thus further high-quality studies are needed to establish causality.

Also according to a recent study, cases were identified that included 40 environmental risk factors and environmental protective factors while the others were associated with genetic factors and peripheral biomarkers.

Alongside these risk factors, however, there are also some protective factors that can help the child limit the outcomes and all the negative consequences of ADHD that we mentioned above.
Among these protective, or mitigating factors, the main ones are:
1) The high educational level of the mother.
2) The good health of the baby shortly after birth.
3) The child's good cognitive skills (particularly language).
4) Family stability.
5) Emotional stability within one's family environment.
With the list of these factors, we end our discussion of ADHD risk factors. In the next section, we'll get into talking about the actual symptoms.

Symptoms of ADHD

Before summarizing and briefly listing all the symptoms that concern ADHD pathology, we need to make a premise. We had already pointed out in the first manual that a disorder such as ADHD does not manifest itself through obvious and clear physical symptoms, but may well be expressed through behavioral problems, problems that can be defined as dysfunctional. What is even more important to underline is that all of these behaviors that can be traced back to ADHD are not unique and objective; on the contrary, they can vary from person to person, making the symptomatology of ADHD completely subjective. There is also to say that the symptoms of attention-deficit/hyperactivity disorder can be of different magnitude. The magnitude can range from mild to severe.

These symptoms then can still exacerbate, worsen, or be a social problem in some settings, particularly in children within their home or school environment. In adults, family, social, and work relationships are the terrains in which typical ADHD symptomatology primarily manifests.

Symptoms in the child: inattention and hyperactivity

Inattention

Briefly analyzing one of the cardinal symptoms of ADHD in the child, which is definitely attention deficit. Present in the denomination of the pathology itself, one of the spheres most affected at the neurological level in the child is precisely the attentional one.

In order to recognize the symptoms of inattention, it is necessary to check, a whole series of general symptoms, which have occurred in a number of not less than six (or more) at least for 6 months with an intensity incompatible with the level of development and has a direct negative impact on social and school/work activities. Among these symptoms we can summarize:

1. The child often fails to pay attention to details. The inattentive person makes distracting errors in schoolwork, at home, or in any other activity. This occurs quite frequently.
2. A child with ADHD often shows quite a bit of difficulty maintaining attention on tasks or play activities.
3. The child does not seem to listen when he/she is spoken to directly and this happens much more frequently than in other children.
4. The child also shows an inability to follow simple instructions and fails to complete schoolwork. Due to inattention, he/she also fails to complete any other activity.
5. Often has difficulty organizing tasks and activities (e.g., difficulty managing sequential tasks; difficulty keeping materials and objects in order; haphazard, disorganized work; manages time poorly, fails to meet deadlines).
6. A child with ADHD will go to great lengths to avoid engaging in tasks that require prolonged mental effort. In addition to avoidance, he or she may show aversion or reluctance to do schoolwork or homework, for example.
7. The person with ADHD is a careless child: he or she often loses items needed for homework or activities (e.g., school

supplies, pencils, books, tools, wallets, keys, papers, glasses, and cell phones).
8. Is often easily distracted by external stimuli, and often daydreams (for older adolescents and adults, incongruous thoughts about the situation may be included).
9. He/she is often careless in daily activities and is also quite clumsy.

Hyperactivity and impulsivity

Regarding the other peculiar aspect of ADHD pathology, namely hyperactivity and impulsivity, the same timelines apply as for inattention: you need to check if six (or more) of the symptoms listed below persist for at least 6 months. Intensity varies depending on developmental level, and the negative impact it can have directly on social and school/work activities (For older adolescents and adults - age 17 and older - at least five symptoms are required).
These symptoms include:
1. Frequent and compulsive waving or clapping of hands and feet.
2. Frequent wiggling in the chair during class or situations where sitting is required.
3. In this regard, those who suffer from hyperactivity leave their seats especially in situations where you should remain seated, resulting in very uncomfortable.
4. He often scurries and jumps into situations where doing so is inappropriate and just as inconvenient.
5. They often feel restless.
6. Children with ADHD are often unable to play or engage in leisurely recreational activities.
7. The child with ADHD, feels very often under pressure, acting as we have already said in this discussion, as if it were "always spring loaded or moved by a motor"
8. He is often overly talkative (talks too much even when he shouldn't).

9. Often fires off an answer before the question has been completed (e.g., completes sentences said by other people; fails to wait their turn in the conversation).
10. He is a very impatient child.
11. Frequently has difficulty waiting his turn (e.g., while waiting in line).
12. Often interrupts others or is intrusive to them (e.g., interrupts conversations, games, or activities; may start using others' things without asking or receiving permission; teens and adults may insert themselves into or take over what others are doing).
13. Frequently poses oppositional and challenging attitudes.

Symptoms in adults

After briefly listing the symptoms of ADHD, here we are refreshing your memory by pointing out all the symptomatology related to the adult with ADHD.

Here are the main symptoms of ADHD in adults are:

- Adult with ADHD experiences quite a few difficulties with concentration and attention. Specifically, these are different forms of chronic inattention. These different forms then translate above all into poor executive capacities (such as, for example, a poor ability to pay and maintain attention for a long time, but also an inability to complete assigned tasks, a propensity to avoid commitments that require a protracted mental effort, an inability to focus on the main theme, etc.).
- State of perpetual restlessness and motor agitation (attributable to hyperactivity). Also the adult subject, as well as the child, has difficulty staying still for a long time in one position.
- Behavioral and Verbal Impulsivity. Even in the adult, impulsivity involves agitation, and presents quite a few difficulties in sitting and standing still. Impulsivity can worsen when the ADHD person often performs acts without thinking about the consequences. These behavioral attitudes can also result in

rudeness when one does not begin to respect turns of phrase within a dialogue, is logorrhoeic, etc..
- Continuous and frequent mood swings.
- Impatience: the ADHD adult may have difficulty waiting their turn (like at a traffic light) and often have episodes where they "lose their temper."
- Time management deficits.
- Low tolerance for frustration.
- Difficulty maintaining interpersonal relationships.
- Disorganization: it translates, in essence, into chaos and lack of randomness in the planning of thought and action.
- Disorganization and difficulty setting priorities and tasks.
- Poor social, interpersonal, and mentalization skills.
- Feeling of boredom and difficulty being satisfied with the performance of one's work or other aspects of daily life.
- Immediate frustration in the face of delaying circumstances.
- Strong emotional lability.
- Difficulty coping with stress or situations in which you find yourself under pressure.

Symptoms in the adult woman

Now we will show you briefly, and even more specifically, what are the symptoms of ADHD, in the adult woman. The review covered all the general symptoms, both in adults and children, but in this case it seems at least obligatory to specify the part that interests us most, namely the adult woman. Recognizing the symptoms, in fact, becomes one of the main steps to dealing with ADHD in the adult woman.

We reiterate that it is only recently that ADHD has received significant and increased attention with regard to its presence in adult women. This is because, as was explained in detail in the first guide, there has always been a widespread belief and perception that ADHD (especially with regard to the hyperactivity component) was a typically, if not exclusively, male disorder. Today, therefore, things have changed a great deal: thanks to the fact that ongoing research has shown an underestimation of the disorder in the female sex, today women are seeing ADHD syndrome fully recognized. The underestimation of ADHD cases in females has long been disallowed because there is a substantial difference at the symptomatic level compared to males. In other words, females are at twice the risk of having ADD, without the "disruptive" symptoms that occur in males. One of these more disruptive symptoms is definitely impulsivity. Basically, it has been the less blatant way females manifest the symptomatology than males, which has often caused them to lack treatment and diagnosis. Scientific evolution, however, has managed to highlight how both sexes are affected by the disorder with the same degree of severity, and suffer the same consequences both professionally and socially. As far as symptoms are concerned, specifically, being many times "repressed", and given the continuous belief that women were excluded from ADHD, they often did not receive a correct diagnosis as children. In fact, there are not a few cases in which women come to consult an expert after ADHD has been diagnosed in one of her children. Many women, therefore, evaluate the presence of ADHD only in conjunction with the genetic component and only then are able to put all the pieces of the puzzle together by recognizing all the symptomatic descriptions of those who have diagnosed behavioral patterns in their children. Having made this long review with so much premise, it is only fair to remind you that, apart from the less marked component of hyperactivity (although girls with ADHD can present strong states of restlessness as well as boys), the symptoms in the adult female differ little from the typical symptoms of children. Although, the sphere of the adult woman is more concerned with the purely humoral sphere, women who suffer from ADHD can in fact experience symptoms linked to a dysphoric mood, anxiety disorders and depression much more frequently than one might imagine. One of the worst situations a woman with ADHD can experience is one related to eating disorders, but not least, also low self-esteem. Because of both possible eating disorders and low self-esteem, symptomatology in women particularly affects the social sphere, where the female subject with ADHD will often tend to isolate herself and have almost no social relationships. With this guide, we will try, in fact, to come to your aid with strategies and advice aimed above all at helping you recover a good relationship, first of all with yourself, and then with others.

Symptomatology in women: a short list

Here is briefly a list of all the possible symptoms found in the adult woman with ADHD:

- Relational and mood problems, with a tendency, as we have already seen above to asociality and isolation.
- Women with ADHD also often suffered from an inability to organize, plan, and manage time. These are individuals who often tend to procrastinate on tasks that need to be done until the last minute. They suffer from forgetfulness, just as often losing needed materials, failing to organize their appointments, and not meeting commitments/deadlines.
- Women will also suffer more from poor time management and sense of time, which results in delays and missed deadlines. For this reason, there will be a special section of the manual dedicated to time management.
- Difficulty managing complex projects.
- Order in the work environment and organization of materials needed for activities.
- Social and relational difficulties.
- Especially in women, therefore, if ADHD is not diagnosed and appropriately treated, with increasing age there will be an increase in difficulties due to comorbidities that, complicating the clinical picture, will require greater intervention and, sometimes priority, to ADHD itself.
- Women with AHDH often feel that their lives are complete "out of control."
- These women often lead very chaotic lives in which economic problems often come up, difficulties in managing work, managing children, organizing the house, and keeping in mind all the commitments of the family and the various errands to be performed-.

- Sexual problems: a woman with ADHD, will have a tendency to have promiscuous relationships or difficulty having sexual intercourse.
- Women with ADHD may have struggled with alcohol and substance abuse, as well as engaging in self-injurious behaviors.
- The symptoms of ADHD, in the adult woman, might go to worsen in a certain period of the month, such as the precycle; in this period we usually notice that thinking is a little less lucid in the woman, compared to other periods. This is all due to the direct impact that ADHD symptoms, such as that of inattention may have on thinking lucidly in a given hormonal period. Also other phases of a woman's life, such as menopause or pregnancy constitute an improvement and a worsening of symptoms. They are also periods when therapy will need to be reviewed as well.

Should you recognize one or more of these symptoms, it is best to see a specialist to resolve the problem as soon as possible. Life with ADHD has already been quite hard for you, so you should not continue to complicate it with a disorder like this. Anyway, now that you are aware of all the common symptoms in women with ADHD, we will briefly pick up the diagnostic process in the next chapter.

Chapter 3: the correct diagnosis in women with ADHD

The diagnosis of ADHD in adults

Without dwelling on the diagnostic process in children with presumed ADHD, we will briefly show you how to ascertain whether you are a possible ADHD subject. If you would like to go into more detail regarding children we refer you to reading the first manual.

In the previous paragraphs, we were able to note that ADHD in adults can manifest with more varied symptoms, but in order to make the diagnosis, it is necessary to identify the presence of the disorder in childhood.

But there's a slight difference with children: while you need 6 or more symptoms to assess for ADHD, you only need 5 symptoms to diagnose ADHD in adults and adolescents aged 17 and older.

Another element to be taken into account is related to the manifestation of symptoms because, as repeatedly stated, the symptoms in adults may appear very different than when they were children. For example, in adults, hyperactivity may appear as extreme restlessness or exhausting others with their activity or their talkativeness.

Other elements to be considered for diagnostic evaluation include a history of somatic and psychiatric treatments and a family history of psychiatric and neurological disorders, given the heritability of the disorder.

Having said that, in order to make a correct diagnosis of ADHD in adults, in addition to taking into account the necessary elements and all related manifestations, it is mandatory, as in the case of children, to consult an expert.

The first step in the concrete discovery of ADH in adults is to see the family physician first and then the psychologist or psychiatrist.

An important element to note is that the diagnosis of ADHD in adulthood follows the exact same pathway as that in childhood. This means that the diagnostic process is the same as that used to diagnose ADHD in both children and adolescents. However, even as regards adults, according to the recommendations of the DSM-IV, to diagnose ADHD it is necessary that there is the equal presence of the three key elements: these elements are always represented by hyperactivity, inattention or impulsivity. In addition to the presence or co-presence of these elements, an assessment will be made of the considerable way in which these symptoms manage to affect two or more contexts of life (such as home, work, and social relationships). A contextualization of the symptomatology is then needed as a second step. As a third step, a further assessment must be made, that is, whether these elements affect social, academic and work functionality and thus the damage they do in these areas. In addition, the manifestations must be chronic, i.e., they must have manifested before the age of 7 years. This is the procedure to be followed. It must be said, however, that each of these diagnostic steps can be, as we have said many times in the first manual but also in this one, even more, complex in the case of adults.

Although more complex, it doesn't mean that ADHD is impossible to diagnose correctly. There is only an even more thorough examination that needs to be done, one that goes beyond the current age group but also includes the period of childhood. In order to ensure that all of these elements can be connected and contextualized, it is necessary to use one of the best tools for assessing a correct diagnosis of ADHD in adults, which is precisely the clinical interview. In this clinical interview, all the areas to be investigated and the elements connected to them are outlined. Areas to be investigated include:

- Marriage.
- Interpersonal relationships.
- Sexual functioning.
- Work functioning.
- Daily activities.
- Parenting and the relationship with children.
- Financial status and management and any legal issues.

Once this screening is done, a so-called "grading scale" is performed. The scale that is generally used for screening includes, in addition to the scale referring to the criteria dictated by the DSM-5, the items of the World Health Organization Adult ADHD Self-Report Scale (ASRS) Symptom Checklist (2005).

The Self-Assessment for a Diagnosis of ADHD

Until now, we have understood that ADHD is a disorder characterized by difficulties in attention in association with hyperactivity and impulsivity.

In adults, it often goes unnoticed by the clinical evaluation, so as to be little if not completely undiagnosed. Symptoms that patients complain about are often related to problems of inattention, difficulties in interpersonal relationships, couples, professional, etc.; however, more and more people are not aware of their disease. Recognizing the symptoms would be of fundamental importance also for the purpose of a preliminary self-evaluation.

In this preliminary self-assessment, you can recognize the most common ADHD symptoms in adults, right before you see a clinician. These symptoms include:

- ✓ Memory Disorders
- ✓ Poor dexterity and repeated errors
- ✓ Impulsivity
- ✓ Mood disorders/substance abuse

Often, adult patients with ADHD may report an excessive tendency to focus on irrelevant or nearly useless details. In addition to this, they have a tendency to develop repetitive or compulsive attempts to control the dysfunction. The diagnosis as we said is complex: clinical evaluations associated with the use of neuropsychological tests are necessary, to be integrated with the collection of information obtained from family members. But doing a preliminary self-assessment could completely pave the way for you: there are several self-assessment tests on the internet that you can take to recognize the possibility of being a subject with ADHD.

Diagnosis in female ADHD

What we have indicated above, is the process that the adult follows in order to correctly diagnose the presence or absence of ADHD. As for the process, the one followed by the woman is identical. The only thing that differs concerns the assessment of symptoms both with regard to the current situation and that of when they were children.

We have already explained to you, and here we refer you to the previous section (and specifically the symptoms in the adult woman), how to assess whether you are a possible case of ADHD. Symptoms in the woman, we repeat differ mainly with regard to the hormonal situation and the hyperactive component. In any case, if more than one symptom is present, in the time frame indicated, then it is advisable that you perform all the necessary checks and have a clinical interview with an expert in ADHD. Specifically regarding the diagnostic check in women, there are a number of different ways in which the symptoms of the disorder are analyzed (identical to ADHD in adults). There are a number of assessments and cognitive tests to determine whether or not you have ADHD. It is only fair to remind you that there is no laboratory testing available for attention-deficit/hyperactivity disorder. Therefore, such a course should be ruled out. Diagnosis is based on completing questionnaires on various behavioral and prior developmental aspects. But, it must be said that an objective examination is also performed and only sometimes, various blood and other tests to exclude other disorders.

Having concluded the explanatory and summarizing part of ADHD, we will explain in the next part of the guide, what are all the therapies used to be able to treat ADHD both for the child, the adult, and specifically for the adult woman.

Part Two- Overview of Effective Therapies for ADHD

Chapter 4: Therapies for ADHD. A little background for the adult woman

What to do if you are diagnosed with ADHD?

In the first manual, there was a special section that covered all the possible risks for a woman diagnosed with ADHD, especially in case of non-treatment. For this reason, we have often recommended that you seek the advice of an expert, but also read the symptoms well in order to guide you in advance toward the discovery of the disease, perhaps by performing some self-assessment tests.

As a first step, after suspecting you have all the symptoms and doing some preliminary testing, you have come to the conclusion that it would be best to do some more specific testing. Another possible scenario might involve the fact that, in addition to all the possible symptoms, you discovered that one of your children suffers from ADHD. Then, associating the genetic component and a few related symptoms you decided to get as correct a diagnosis as possible. In the latter case, you are pretty much certain that you have ADHD. So, after going through the whole process of being diagnosed, you have found out that you are a subject with ADHD disorder.

Now what to do if you have found out you have a positive ADHD diagnosis?

First of all, as we have said many times, it is not the end of the world and there is no need to panic, since it is not an irreversible disease, although the risks of not treating it are still high.

In addition to not panicking, the really important thing is to get informed. Being informed about each type of treatment and which one is best for you, is the expert's job.

One behavior you should absolutely avoid, in addition to panic, would be isolation. You do not pose a lethal danger to those around you, but it is best to surround yourself with people who can support you on the path to ADHD resolution.

As we will see in the next chapter of this guide, there are different treatment protocols and different approaches that are planned and implemented for the treatment of ADHD. All of these protocols, however, are designed to reduce the severity of symptoms and to promote good inclusion in general, not only of the child, but also of the woman in her living environment. In the adult woman, specifically, it aims to resolve all those problems that affect disorganization, time management, and the elimination of "toxic" behaviors associated with this pathology.

The objective of this treatment is to develop adequate well-being that also depends on relationships and their quality. Relationships occur between the child and parents, but also with teachers, while the adult is towards the home environment and external relationships.

However, for the woman, in particular, who has discovered that she has ADHD, it is necessary to plan a specific and personalized treatment. Planning a personalized treatment means, above all, adapting the therapy according to the social situation in which she finds herself. It is a matter, as we will also say later, of shaping the treatment according to one's specific needs, symptoms, and repercussions in professional, social, and family life.

When it comes to discussing specific therapy, and then planning it in the most correct way possible, the clinician must keep in mind several factors that determine a certain therapeutic choice, including the comorbidity of the woman with ADHD, her family situation, socioeconomic level, previous school experiences, possible work situation, as well as the possibility of going to the therapeutic referral service.

This was the general course of action to take if you found out you had an ADHD diagnosis.

In the next section we will specifically outline everything there is to know about a new ADHD diagnosis for the adult female. The concept of multimodal therapy will also be mentioned. A concept that will be taken up and expanded upon in the next section of the book.

Diagnosis of ADHD in adult women: what you need to know

We stated in the previous paragraph that in case you have been diagnosed with ADHD, one of the most important things to do is definitely to get informed.

Learn about the genesis, evolution, symptoms and diagnosis of the disease, but above all about the risks associated with this disease. And for this we refer you to a thorough reading of the first manual. What you need to know specifically in this section of our second text is that the treatment of this pathology does not have an unambiguous and precise protocol, but the treatment protocol is much more complex than you might imagine. Whether it's for the child themselves, the adult, or you specifically, the ideal treatment and approach to combating ADHD are multimodal. By multimodal, and we will elaborate on this in the next chapter, we are referring to treatment that involves multiple actors and multiple environmental areas.

The ideal approach and subsequent treatment for attention deficit hyperactivity syndrome therefore take place on several fronts, involving not only the patient himself, but also external environments (such as school and work) and especially the family. This involvement, in the multimodal mode, must be interspersed with pharmacological intervention.

Another aspect of multimodal therapy also concerns the application of interventions involving psychosocial aspects. The cognitive and behavioral tradition has allowed the development of some educational and therapeutic programs that are also suitable for adult women. It is important that you dwell on this point because one thing that is really essential to know is that, in the case of ADHD, the path will not be simple and therapy, as per protocol, is not always suitable for every case of ADHD.

So know that your path needs to be, planned, specific and multimodal.

Attention deficit hyperactivity disorder is a chronic condition that can therefore be addressed with different approaches. It is indeed possible to use medication, psychotherapy, education, lifestyle changes, or a combination of them. But it is still a rather subjective therapy.

Your specific case must be studied, and planned according to your symptoms and the evolution of the disease.

Therefore, the most important thing to do is to never accept a standard therapy or protocol. Standard therapy is not acceptable if it has not taken all the specific aspects into consideration. Another important thing you need to know is that the main goal of all these targeted interventions is to reduce the symptoms of ADHD and improve the dysfunctions that the condition entails. And consequently to make your life better.

Remember that it is very important, although the picture may improve with time, that you can intervene immediately, after discovering the diagnosis. Unfortunately, in the case of adult women, this pathology has already been neglected for too long; therefore, it is not the case of still letting this pathology negatively affect your existence.

Chapter 5: Pharmacological therapies for the child with ADHD.

A little background: one-on-one, multimodal treatment for ADHD

In this chapter we are going to tell you in detail what the approaches and protocols used to be able to treat a child with ADHD. We first tell you that attention deficit hyperactivity disorder (ADHD) can be treated with psychotherapy or with a combination of medication and psychotherapy (as we had mentioned to you in the previous chapter i.e. multimodal treatment). Regarding this multimodal approach, several randomized controlled trials have been able to show that behavioral therapies and drug therapy are less effective when used individually for school-aged children, but behavioral or combination therapy is recommended for younger children and is significantly more effective.

But as we said in the previous chapter, each case of ADHD has unique and different characteristics that must be treated with individual strategies. This is true for women, but also for children. Therapy, in fact, must be designed and shaped directly on the child, and must be aimed at helping them control their impulsive, inattentive behaviors and acquire problem solving skills. Skills, as we have seen, are almost completely lacking in children with ADHD. In this regard, a key concept that you will need to keep in mind at all times is that ADHD treatment acts on the manifestations of ADHD but does not remove the root causes, which, as we have explained to you many times, are related to the birth and genetics of the individual with ADHD. Through these one-on-one ADHD treatments, the child must learn to manage each emotion in a balanced way, thus mitigating the most dysfunctional symptoms and behaviors. Through therapy, he is helped to recognize the nature of his emotionality and replace negative impulses with more positive expressions. The goal is to learn to motivate his actions and avoid acting without thinking.

Treatments for ADHD are of fundamental importance to improve the social and behavioral aspects of the child's life. The goal we said above, is precisely to mitigate the main symptoms such as impulsivity and poor concentration. It also seeks, in other words, to improve his school learning and relationships with peers.

Solving all these problems still represents a huge obstacle for a child with ADHD. It is necessary to point him in the right direction, making him understand the origin of the problem and helping him to find different possible solutions. Progress is evident when he is independently able to make the correct choice.

Let's learn together about the main treatment method used for children with ADHD.

Drug therapy

Let's look at the first type of treatment, namely pharmacological treatment. When it comes to drug therapy, psychostimulants, specifically, are considered the most effective medications for adolescents, children, and adults with ADHD. This is definitely the most drastic and impactful form of treatment for ADHD symptomatology.

Although medications do not completely correct the neurophysiological differences of patients with attention-deficit/hyperactivity disorder, they are effective in alleviating their symptoms and allowing the patient to participate in activities and tasks that were previously impossible due to poor attention and impulsivity. Medications allow control of abnormal behaviors thus enhancing cognitive behavioral interventions, motivation and self-esteem. There are two types of medications that are used, namely those that are stimulant and those that are non-stimulant. Let's look specifically at what these are.

Stimulant drugs

Let's first go over stimulant medications, how they work, how they are dosed, and all the possible side effects. Stimulant drugs usually used to treat ADHD include methylphenidate (Ritalin), amphetamines (Adderal), and dextroamphetamine (Dextrostat, Dexedrine). Psychostimulant drugs represented by methylphenidate or amphetamine salts are the most widely used. The main positive results due to the use of them, concern purely the maintenance of attention levels, and greater control of impulsivity and hyperactivity.

The positive response, however, as with all drugs, varies from subject to subject. Even the dosage is very subjective: it depends both on the severity of the symptoms and on the tolerability of the patient towards the drug. The dosage, in fact, is modified according to frequency and quantity. This modulation must change until the optimal balance between response and adverse effects is reached. As for always stimulant drugs, methylphenidate is usually used starting with 0.3 mg/kg orally 1 time daily (this is the so-called immediate-release form), and increased weekly in frequency. This frequency increase typically results in a shift in intake from 1 to about 2 to 3 times per day or every 4 h during waking hours. It must also be said that many clinicians try the dosage taken in the morning and middle hours of the day. They believe, in fact, that this is the time when methylphenidate has the most effect. This is, in fact, still empirical evidence. The dosage can be increased when the results are not satisfactory, but the drug is still quite well tolerated. Most children achieve an optimal balance between benefits and adverse effects at doses between 0.3 and 0.6 mg/kg. The dextrorotatory isomer of methylphenidate is the active half and is available for prescription for half the dose.

The dosage schemes of stimulant drugs in general can in fact be modulated and adjusted to cover specific days and times (to give a practical example, during school hours and homework). It is possible to try pharmacological breaks especially during weekends, vacations, or during summer vacations. Moving from dosage to effects, Treatment with this stimulant medication aims to stabilize the behavioral attitudes characteristic of ADHD, such as moderate to severe distraction, time-limited attention span, hyperactivity, emotional lability, and impulsivity. It has been demonstrated, in fact, that methylphenidate is effective in about 70% of patients. With regard to the timing of results, already after the first week of treatment observed positive effects on attention span, hyperactivity, and improvement in social interactions and relationships.

Moving from methylphenidate to dextroamphetamine too has a fairly gradual intake process. It is usually started (often in combination with racemic amphetamines) at 0.15 to 0.2 mg/kg orally 1 time per day, which can then be increased to 2 or 3 times per day or every 4 h during waking hours. Single doses of 0.15 to 0.4 mg/kg are usually provided. Despite single doses, in fact, they are usually effective. Dosage and posology, again, must be balanced against side effects; actual doses vary significantly among individuals, but, in general, higher doses increase the likelihood of unacceptable adverse effects. In general, the dosage of dextroamphetamine is about two-thirds that of methylphenidate.

For both methylphenidate and dextroamphetamine, once their optimal dosage is identified they will then be prescribed and used in extended release at the same dose, to avoid the need to administer the drugs, for example, at school. Long-release formulations are in substances of matrix wax tablets, biphasic capsules containing the equivalent of 2 doses, and osmotic-release pills and transdermal patches that allow coverage for up to 12 h. Recently, short- and long-acting liquid preparations have also become available. In any case, these are drugs that, acting over the long term, have equally long-lasting effects on the control of ADHD symptoms. Pure dextroamphetamine preparations (e.g., dexmethylphenidate) are often used to minimize adverse effects such as those associated with anxiety; they are usually administered in doses of about half that of mixed preparations. Propharmaceutical preparations, on the other hand, are prescribed and used for their unique characteristics, such as slow release, longer duration of action, fewer adverse effects, and lower potential for abuse. Thanks, however, to the slow release it is possible to notice the positive effects, especially at school: the improvement in learning is obtained, in fact, with low doses. It is the behavioral improvement that often makes low dosages: in fact, it usually requires higher doses of these drugs.

On the other hand, as far as a placebo is concerned, the periods in which it is administered (usually ranging from 5 to 10 school days to be sure of the reliability of the observations) are indicated to evaluate the real need or not of the drug.

Let's get down to the nitty gritty, which is the side, or adverse, effects. Like all drugs, in fact, stimulant drugs can have contraindications. Common adverse effects of stimulant drugs may include:

- ✓ Sleep disorders and insomnia
- ✓ Headache
- ✓ Gastralgia
- ✓ Appetite reduction
- ✓ Tachycardia and high blood pressure
- ✓ Many studies then managed to prove that average growth in height slows within 2 years precisely because of the use of stimulant drugs, and the slowdown apparently persists into adulthood with chronic use of such drugs.

There are also less common adverse effects, such as depression. Depression, in fact, can often represent an inability to shift attention easily (hyper concentration). This can manifest as depressed behavior (sometimes families describe the child's behavior as very dull, even zombie-like) rather than actual clinical depression. In fact, stimulant medications are even used as an adjunctive treatment for depression. In any case, if depressive behavior does occur, it can sometimes be resolved either by reducing the dose of the stimulant medication or by trying another medication.

Non-stimulant drugs

In addition to stimulant medications, atomoxetine (specialty drug Strattera), a selective norepinephrine reuptake inhibitor, is often used to treat ADHD. Atomoxetine is a non-stimulant drug belonging to the class of selective norepinephrine reuptake inhibitors. The drug is found to be quite effective in treating the main symptoms of

ADHD in children, but data on its efficacy compared to stimulant medications are mixed.

Regarding its dosage, The usual starting dose is 0.5 mg/kg orally 1 time/day, escalated to 1.2 to 1.4 mg/kg weekly. The long half-life allows administration 1 time/day, although it requires continuous use to be effective. The maximum recommended daily dose is 100 mg. Typically, however, we tell you that atomoxetine is administered in a single daily dose based on body weight.

These types of non stimulant drugs also have side effects. Among these side effects, some children have shown nausea, sedation, irritability, and rage; rarely, however, very serious adverse effects such as high liver toxicity and suicidal ideation may occur.

Antidepressant selective norepinephrine reuptake inhibitors are sometimes used in cases where psychostimulants are ineffective: these selective inhibitors include bupropion and venlafaxine, alpha-2 agonists such as clonidine and guanfacine, and other psychoactive medications; they can also be used in cases where psychostimulants show serious adverse effects, although they are less effective and are not recommended as first-line drugs. Sometimes these drugs are used in combination with stimulants for synergistic effects. Regardless, it is always critically important to evaluate adverse effects in a child with ADHD. The greatest concern for the treatment of attention-deficit/hyperactivity disorder stems primarily from adverse drug interactions. Indeed, reviewing potential drug interactions turns out to be an important part of the pharmacological management of children, but also of patients in general, with attention-deficit/hyperactivity disorder.

Intuniv and EMA

In addition, the EMA (European Medicines Agency), through the CHMP (Committee for Medicinal Products for Human Use), has given a positive opinion for the granting of marketing authorization under the centralized procedure for another drug for ADHD, Intuniv (guanfacine), for children and adolescents (age 6-17 years) for whom standard drug therapy (stimulants) has proven to be non-resolving and not tolerated.

The CHMP also established that Intuniv must, however, be an integral part of a therapeutic plan including psycho-behavioral therapies, in addition to pharmacological ones, supervised by a specialist. Intuniv, in essence, contains the active ingredient guanfacine, which is an antagonist of alpha-2 adrenergic receptors: in fact, it serves to activate mechanisms in particular areas of the brain capable of promoting attention, organization and impulse control. This mechanism is different from classical therapy for ADHD. Moreover, the improvement of some parameters of this type of disorder that correlate with the reduction of symptoms, has been observed by as many as 13 clinical studies in patients treated with guanfacine, which led to the formulation of the positive opinion by the CHMP. Side effects observed with guanfacine included: bradycardia, hypotension, fainting, drowsiness, sedation, increased risk of falls and accidents, and weight gain. The adverse effects of this type of medication are still being studied and analyzed.

Conclusions on drug therapy

Pharmacological therapy is one of the most widely used means of treating the most negative effects of ADHD in children. It must also be said that, in order for there to be lasting improvements over time, it is rather important to flank pharmacological treatment with a combined course of cognitive and behavioral strategies that help the child, parents and teachers to reach a full understanding of the problem and in the management of the problematic behaviors present. In essence, multimodal therapy is needed.

Although the effectiveness of pharmacological treatment has been widely demonstrated, through numerous clinical trials, the best results in the treatment of attention-deficit hyperactivity disorder are obtained by combining pharmacological therapy with psycho-behavioral therapies such as parent training, child training, and teacher counseling. We will examine these treatments in more detail in the next chapter: here, in brief, we tell you that parents are taught what ADHD is and how to apply behavioral strategies (such as how to organize their child's day, how to behave when excessive episodes of hyperactivity and impulsivity occur, how to help them keep everything in order, cope with a task and simplify those that are too complex; they are also taught how to impose clear rules to be followed and how to reward or punish them when these rules are broken). Parent training also helps parents deal with the stress and frustration that can result from all the issues involved in raising a child with ADHD. Systematic counseling for teachers, on the other hand, serves to help them adopt a constructive attitude toward their child with ADHD and structure the classroom environment to meet his or her needs.

This concludes our discussion of medication therapy for the child with ADHD. In the next chapter, we will look at behavioral therapy and all the repercussions that can result for a child with ADHD.

Chapter 6: Psycho-Behavioral Therapy for the Child with ADHD.

Psycho-behavioral treatment

After talking about the possible pharmacological treatment suitable for the child with ADHD, we now move on to explain psycho-behavioral therapy. Psycho-behavioral therapy, along with pharmacological therapy, is one of the most widely used treatments regarding the child with ADHD disorder. It includes a whole set of techniques and exercises that aim at the acquisition of the child's skills of self-control and immediate response to external stimuli and problems.

But beware: this is not an approach that involves only the child; the therapeutic process also includes the active participation of both parents and teachers. This active participation is aimed at implementing the right approach to the child in order to correct him/her with equally appropriate interventions. In other words, it is part of that multimodal strategy that acts on several fronts that we have often mentioned.

Behavioral therapy or counseling

Counseling, which includes cognitive-behavioral therapy (which could, in turn, include approaches such as goal-setting, self-monitoring, modeling, and imitation), has often been very effective for the child with ADHD, as it has helped him not only to understand the attention-deficit/hyperactivity disorder but especially on the possibilities of dealing with it and how to do it. It is a therapy that is in fact, based on respect for rules and routine.

While drug therapy is based on subjective choices that aim at the most ideal balance possible between dosage, positive response and adverse effects, cognitive-behavioral therapy with the child is a completely individual therapy designed and shaped on the needs and symptoms presented by the child with ADHD. In fact, this type of therapy's main purpose is to modify problem behaviors. In addition to modifying problem behaviors, this approach is aimed at monitoring the actions of the child with ADHD, controlling his anger and emotional regulation, conscious and non-impulsive actions, and increasing his social skills. Being a completely subjective path, therefore, the therapist will use specific behavioral strategies designed for the individual subject with this disorder, starting with the analysis of problematic behaviors in various contexts, focusing especially on the consequences of these behaviors and actions. This analysis is done in order to structure an intervention aimed at decreasing the occurrence of problematic behaviors and negative actions that compromise both the school and social context of the child. In addition, through the teaching of social skills and emotional management, the child will also learn to relate better and interact with their peers by respecting the rules, waiting their turn, playing and sharing games, asking for help, learning and reading and understanding the tone and expression of others to understand their emotional state and respond appropriately. Basically, it is a process of re-education of all those inappropriate behaviors we talked about in the first manual and taken up in the previous chapters.

Unlike always a pharmacological intervention, a cognitive-behavioral approach, therefore, focuses more on directly teaching the child self-control skills and problem-solving skills. Areas of focus, therefore, include impulsivity and self-control (such as anger management, and the use of non-aggressive problem-solving techniques).

In terms of therapy with the clinician, in summary, the child with ADHD syndrome undergoes targeted sessions, which are geared towards helping him overcome his difficulties in concentration, achieve specific goals, and not be distracted by his surroundings. His positive behaviors are rewarded to improve his self-esteem and incentivize their repetition. The same goes for more impulsive or hyperactive behaviors.

Even classroom behavior is improved through this approach: even if we will specify more in the next paragraphs, teachers also play a key role in this counseling therapy: they can intervene, for example, by reducing all those noisy and visual environmental stimuli, or by giving tasks of appropriate duration, also address paths of emotional training.

Therefore, we can affirm that the most lasting improvements in behavioral type are obtained by placing side by side the therapy at home and in the classroom, just a cognitive-behavioral program composed of all these techniques and cognitive and behavioral strategies able to help children, parents and teachers to understand and how to manage problematic behaviors. Of fundamental importance, therefore, are the paths to be taken in parallel to the cognitive-behavioral treatment of the child, such as Parent Training and Teacher Training. Below we will explain more about what these are.

Parent training

Parent training represents another fundamental aspect of psycho-behavioral therapy for a child with ADHD. This type of approach also involves the parents, who must be informed about the characteristics of ADHD and its consequences. This represents the first phase of this type of therapy. This first phase of information is in fact called parent education, as it serves to teach parents how to understand ADHD, and how to interpret the consequent actions of the child who is subject to this disorder. This knowledge serves to make them more aware of their child's situation and learn how to help him or her in a constructive way, and above all to achieve the goal of alleviating less appropriate behavior, even at home.

Subsequently to the information phase, the therapeutic path can take over and, consequently, be integrated with the real parent training. This second phase, represents, in fact, the best tool to teach them the appropriate behavioral strategies to follow.

Through Parent Training, parents are taught useful strategies for children to be more reflective, more consistent in educational practices, and more organized and structured in the family environment, in order to reduce problem behaviors and foster the child's self-management skills.

It's not just about discipline and self-management: reward can also play a key role in incentivizing a child with ADHD to achieve his or her goals. In fact, adding incentives and rewards helps with behavior management and is often effective in further motivating the child. Once modes of action and limits for the child are established, coupled with the fact that parents have mastered management techniques, children are often better cared for at home, especially those with attention-deficit/hyperactivity disorder where hyperactivity and poor impulse control are prevalent.

In other words, intervention programs directed at parents aim to increase awareness and knowledge of ADHD, not only on the part of parents but also in the child. Parent training also serves to develop the ability of the parents themselves to manage ADHD, modifying through these strategies all the dysfunctional behaviors enacted in the relationship with the child. The main focus of the intervention is therefore centered on the development of greater reflective skills by parents, to help them acquire greater consistency and stability in their educational strategies that help and support the child in the acquisition of the ability to self-manage. Other management strategies for ADHD include feeding diets that include the exclusion of certain foods, vitamin supplements, antioxidants, or other compounds, and nutritional or biochemical interventions (which, however, have shown less effectiveness). Regarding nutrition and lifestyles best suited to deal with ADHD, we refer you to the next section of the text.

A fundamental role is played by the promotion of a better emotional climate in the family and more effective communication with the child, also by better defining limits and rules to be followed.

Up to this point, we have shown you the best strategies for parent training, but we need to pay attention to one detail: it is true that parents are key players in the management of ADHD, but it is only through cooperation with teachers that psycho-behavioral therapy can be 100% effective. Through Teacher Training, as we will see below, guidance will be provided to teachers on how to structure and organize the school environment tailored to the child with ADHD. This reorganization of the school environment takes place considering the specific characteristics and needs of the child, in order to improve the child's ability to pay attention and motivate him/her to learn and foster relationships with his/her peers (in this case, classmates).

In the family environment and in the school environment, it can be useful to adopt an educational system such as the "Token Economy". In this system, both the child and the adults (parents/teachers) mutually commit to a contract. This sort of contract is agreed upon and determined by both parties, and foresees the assignment of a token for each correct behavior on the part of the child; while, on the contrary, the non-assignment of a token or even the loss of the token already assigned may occur in the case of incorrect behavior. When a certain number of tokens is reached (previously established in the contract) the child will receive the prize, chosen and indicated by the same. This mechanism serves purely to encourage the commitment and motivation of the child, in order for him to understand the importance of modifying his own inappropriate behavior. In other words, it is about incentives for the child with ADHD to self-discipline.

These methods of reorganization and rewards are inevitably interconnected with the home environment, as the child's home should prove to be a natural extension of the behavioral strategies implemented in the classroom. Therefore, teachers must be supportive of ADHD management, including parental support.

When difficulties persist at home, parents should in fact be encouraged by teachers to seek professional assistance from specialists, and supported in exercising behavioral management techniques.

How does parent training work?

Having explained in general how parent training works, we will now turn to give you a better understanding of how it works. So far, we have been able to understand that the problems related to the behavior of the child, but also of the ADHD adolescent make it necessary to involve the parents in the treatment process. This is because we cannot just pin our hopes on a miracle cure, but we need a multimodal approach that sees the family as the protagonist since it represents a fundamental resource for encouraging the appearance of positive behaviors. Unfortunately, in addition to medication, not even parental love alone is sufficient, as it is not able to deal with all the problems produced by ADHD on an individual basis, and without appropriate support and strategies will not succeed in modifying the dysfunctional behaviors of the child affected by the disorder. Parents will be encouraged and helped to cope with the symptoms of the disorder, and to structure an environment that can promote the self-regulation and self-discipline of the child. In the Parent Training approach, a series of individual or group meetings are scheduled. This will be determined depending on the preferences of the individuals involved, and the needs of the child with ADHD. Either way, these meetings will include:

- ✓ Provide all correct information regarding the difficulties of the child with ADHD. It will be mentioned, also as all possible treatments.
- ✓ Clarify the goals of the intervention in general and the individual goals to be achieved.
- ✓ Identify dysfunctional attributes and modes of interaction. After identifying them, a process of reframing is provided.
- ✓ Identified the positive strengths of the child/adolescent. These strengths will be used to increase the frequency of improved behaviors through positive reinforcement techniques.
- ✓ Contextualized all problem behaviors so as to recognize the importance of antecedents and the consequences they entail.
- ✓ Show all the ways in which you can create a predictable environment with clear rules that are well understood and shared. This predictable environment is intended to facilitate the management of the child/adolescent's behavior.
- ✓ Teach all appropriate problem behavior management techniques and problem solving strategies.

Parent Training, as we said above, can be carried out in individual sessions (in which the participation of both parents is preferable) or in groups. It provides for approximately 12 meetings that are repeated every 15 days. Each scheduled meeting will last about 90 minutes, and within it, parents will have a real opportunity to change their vision of their child and themselves within the parental relationship. Moreover, they will be able to transform all the dysfunctional vicious circles into functional interactions that will increase their child's strengths. From all the explanations shown to you above, it is easy to deduce that attending these meetings becomes of paramount importance not only to improve the condition of the child or adolescent with ADHD but to ensure that the parents can have the right support to best meet this challenge.

School-based interventions for the child with ADHD: Teacher Training

Teachers, as we said, together with parents, are direct protagonists in the management of the behaviors of children with ADHD. Like parents, they must first of all face an informative process. In fact, they must learn all the best assessment techniques suitable for cases of ADHD, teaching and behavioral strategies according to their needs. In addition, teachers must be prepared to improve the inclusion of individuals with ADHD in their classes. Finally, they must also know, as we said in the previous paragraph, the best methods for organizing the school environment and, above all, understand that the child suffers from a specific disorder that leads him to have behaviors, even if not always appropriate, that do not lead him to intentionally create problems.

The typically informative intervention is in fact aimed at directing teachers towards a deeper knowledge of the disorder, first providing them with all the information necessary to reach a full understanding of the ADHD disorder, and then acting as a basis so that they can begin to recognize the positive aspects of the child, despite the difficulties that this disorder entails.

From this point of view, it becomes rather central to provide teachers with information on the structuring of the school environment. This structuring has as a main requirement the fact that it must take into account the needs and characteristics of the hyperactive child, in order to enhance his attentional skills and learning. Moreover, teachers must be provided with useful strategies to manage and modify dysfunctional behaviors, as well as to improve relationships with peers.

It must be said that it is often not easy for teachers to manage a situation in which a child with ADHD is present: in fact, they often live with a perpetual state of anxiety that lasts throughout the lesson. This anxiety concerns the fear they have for the safety of the classmates of the child with ADHD, who may be the object of his or her impulsiveness. It is advisable, above all in order to avoid problems of this kind, that they also know and actively follow the therapeutic treatment, in order to manage the situation in a functional way. If action is taken not only on the child, but also on his environment with the help of family members and teachers, the results are evident from the first sessions.

How does teacher training work?

After explaining what is meant by teacher training, we will briefly explain how this approach that sees the involvement of teachers in the management of the subject with ADHD works. We have already noted that including teacher training in the treatment of ADHD is an integral and essential part of a therapeutic pathway for the treatment of the child with ADHD. It is another piece of what we have already called a "multimodal approach". School is usually the environment in which the dysfunctional behaviors of ADHD are most evident because hyperactivity, impulsivity and inattention compromise the child's ability to respect the rules of the classroom. In addition to preventing the child from respecting class rules, ADHD heavily affects the child's level of learning, preventing him or her from achieving appreciable academic results consistent with their intellectual potential. Teacher Training, therefore, is an intervention that must be carried out in conjunction with Parent Training and aims to encourage self-regulation, self-control and self-awareness of one's own behavior in the child/adolescent with ADHD within the school environment. This other piece of the multimodal therapeutic approach is expressed through:
- ✓ Increased awareness of the difficulties that the child/adolescent with ADHD disorder encounters on a daily basis, but also of all

those situations that can be linked to their problematic behaviors.
- ✓ Writing and establishing school rules and routines, including organizing materials.
- ✓ The implementation of specific behavior modification techniques within the classroom.
- ✓ A classroom and environment setting will minimize the occurrence of problem behaviors.
- ✓ Improved communication from both teachers and parents.
- ✓ Recovery and improvement especially in the relationship that intercedes between teacher and child, are often challenged by the difficulties of behavior management.

Teacher Training is critical at this point to achieve improvement in the ADHD child/adolescent's school behavior and learning. Three to four meetings can be scheduled over the course of the school year. All of these meetings should be planned according to the needs of the individual case, always remembering that each case is specific and, consequently should be treated subjectively to the purpose and needs of the child with ADHD. Also in this regard, training courses can also be organized upon request, especially in school environments in countries where ADHD is not yet well known. In any case, the intervention of the teacher is also very important so that the child receives continuity of treatment after setting it up at home with parent training.

Intervention with the child

With regard to ADHD, in addition to clinician, parent, and teacher intervention, direct interventions with children are absolutely necessary as well.

In the past, but still today, we have seen that many approaches aimed at working with children with ADHD have been cognitive-behavioral in orientation and have emphasized the teaching of self-control skills. One example procedure that can be applied to manage impulsive behavior is called self-instruction. This type of procedure is primarily used to dampen the impulsivity factor. This approach, in practice, consists of instructing children with ADHD to use "self-talk" strategies through a technique that divides problem-solving into various steps and objectives (identifying a problem, generating alternatives, choosing, implementing, and evaluating a solution). The hypothesis is that these self-talk techniques, initially put into practice in an obvious way, can be perfectly internalized by the child and could compensate for deficits in self-control. The specific training then uses all of the techniques of anger control. Anger control, in turn, represents another self-management strategy, whereby children are taught how to recognize internal (physiological) signals of increased anger, how to develop techniques to decrease or otherwise direct anger (move away from the situation), and how to use these techniques in response to the provocations of others.

Cognitive-behavioral therapy in interaction with the child with ADHD is aimed not only at controlling impulsivity but also in a synergistic manner towards all areas implicated in the disorder and deficient. The child is taught strategies that serve to systematically guide him/her in planning his/her behavior in the various areas of life and in problem-solving (Problem Solving strategies). It is also focused on the acquisition of the ability to monitor their actions, developing a capacity for self-regulation towards impulsivity and inattention.

Intervention is also aimed at increasing social skills, through compliance with rules, the development of more effective interactions, and the ability to decode one's control status.

The child also learns to draw important information from his mistakes in order to "self-correct", but also to know how to reward himself for achieving positive results. As a result, he will feel motivated to behave appropriately in order to receive a reward not only through the external environment but also from himself.

However, we can briefly summarize what are the main objectives of direct therapeutic intervention with the child/adolescent. These main objectives aimed:

- ✓ To teach precise techniques of self-control, anger management, and problem-solving
- ✓ To the improvement of impulsive and inappropriate behaviors

- ✓ To improve interpersonal relationships with parents, teachers, siblings and peers
- ✓ To the improvement of learning skills
- ✓ To increase autonomy and self-esteem.

Conclusions on psycho-behavioral therapy

ADHD in children can be treated not only with targeted medications but also with environmental interventions (such as those at school or at home) that assume that if the skills required to regulate behavior are deficient, then these skills should be directly taught or developed. From the point of view of social learning, teaching children specific skills involving "self-regulation" is often primarily the task of parental education (parent training) and then of teachers. However, it is especially useful to reward appropriate behavior and punish inappropriate behavior, so that the child becomes increasingly aware of how to adapt his behavior to the school and social context, despite the enormous difficulties he encounters every day. These types of treatment aim to directly improve behavior, as they act on the child's current behaviors and environmental characteristics that affect the child.

In order to achieve these results, and especially to make them last, other kinds of treatments and forms of support are needed, which many clinicians recommend being used along with pharmacological treatment, which, as we have seen, are a parent and teacher training.

In conclusion, to date, the best treatment for attention deficit hyperactivity disorder is the multimodal type. By multimodal, as we have already explained in the course of this discussion, we mean an approach that provides a combination of pharmacological, psychoeducational and psychotherapeutic interventions. For decades, especially in the United States, medications have been used to specifically treat the symptoms of ADHD. However, it has often been noted that on their own they are not enough, but that a multifunctional approach is also needed to affect the psychological and behavioral sphere of the child with ADHD. Not to mention that they often cause more adverse reactions than benefits.

On their own then, medications cannot help make children with ADHD feel inwardly better or provide those specific coping skills they need. They cannot even be able to teach them specific social skills or increase motivation. And this is where psycho-behavioral approaches have to step in, because only with these approaches can comprehensive help be provided so that the child with ADHD can not only feel better or self-discipline, but reintegrate into a normal life context, as all children deserve at this stage of their existence. More precisely, as demonstrated by the study carried out by the MTA (an acronym for Multimodal Treatment Study of Children with ADHD), the key symptoms of ADHD, such as inattention, hyperactivity and impulsivity, will be best managed, in the most serious symptomatic cases, by pharmacological therapy, while any associated disorders, especially conduct and learning disorders, as well as problems with social interaction, will mostly require psychosocial and psychoeducational therapies. Therapies that, as we have seen, are entirely family, school and child-centered. Therapeutic interventions of a psychological nature, in fact, should aim at improving children's interpersonal relationships with their parents, siblings, teachers and peers, decreasing inadequate behavior, improving school learning (quantity and quality of knowledge, method of study), increasing the sense of self-esteem and autonomy in the various spheres of social life. In essence, it is about improving the quality of life of ADHD children and adolescents, including through understanding and social acceptability of the disorder. We must therefore not make them feel wrong, but always try to meet them with concrete help from everyone.

This concludes our comprehensive analysis of all treatments suitable for the child and adolescents diagnosed with ADHD. Instead, in the next chapter, we will look at what treatments are best suited for women with ADHD.

Chapter 7: The Effective Therapies for the Woman with ADHD.

A multimodal approach also for the adult woman with ADHD

In the first textbook, two possible approaches for woman with ADHD were specified. In this specific section of the second text, however, we will take care to indicate, just as we did for the child with ADHD in the previous chapters, what are the pieces of the ideal multimodal approach for the adult woman suffering from this disorder. This is because, even in the case of a diagnosis of ADHD for the adult woman, we will primarily indicate a multimodal treatment that acts on multiple fronts. So, treatment in the adult woman involves a combination of pharmacological and non-pharmacological treatments. Specifically, non-pharmacological treatment includes cognitive behavioral therapy and specific training programs aimed at having the individual develop effective strategies to minimize the negative impact of the disorder in daily life. The only difference with treatment in adolescents and children is that teacher training is not provided as it cannot be counted among the main environments in which adult women with ADHD operate.

Another very important aspect to emphasize and reiterate before concluding this premise is that, since ADHD affects each person differently, what is most effective for most patients, even in adult women, is a combination of targeted, personalized and ad hoc treatments. However, there are no standard treatments but multi-pronged treatments centered on individual needs, including psychoeducation, pharmacological treatment, and psychological support. Let's look specifically at what each of these approaches consists of in the next few paragraphs.

Drug therapy in women with ADHD

Pharmacological therapy could be one of the elements for resolving, we remind you, not ADHD itself and its causes, but to mitigate the symptomatic situations that we showed you in the first manual that concern adult women with ADHD. But, before illustrating to you what the pharmacological possibilities are, it is only fair to emphasize that on their own, even in the case of the adult female, medication is not enough. In fact, treatment with medication only acts as a support in the management of symptoms but does not provide for a total remission of the same.

Although it must be said that many adult individuals, including women, show clear improvements in the most adverse situations with the pharmacological treatment provided for the disorder. In fact, pharmacological treatment is fundamental in working on the nuclear symptoms of ADHD: as we will see below, the most studied and most effective pharmacological treatment is that based on stimulants (methylphenidate and dexamphetamine). Although the efficacy of stimulants in the treatment of ADHD in adults is recognized, their role is still controversial and studied, which is why there is talk of a multi-pronged approach to dealing with ADHD in adults as well.

To cite a few statistics, although 25-50% of adults treated with medications (especially stimulant medications) show improvement in the nuclear symptoms of the disorder, they nevertheless have residual difficulties in several areas of functioning, i.e., school, work, some skills such as driving, or in social relationships. In fact, improvement in nuclear symptoms does not necessarily correspond with an improvement in the person's overall functioning.

In fact, the effectiveness of comprehensive, multimodal treatment includes psycho-education on the disorder, psychological therapy, and social skills training. All of these should be combined with possible drug therapy, which should be carefully studied with your clinician.

There is also another very important aspect to emphasize: pharmacological therapy, in addition to not being used as the only therapy, represents an alternative, and not a primary choice, especially for women with ADHD. Before resorting to pharmacological treatment, in fact, psycho-behavioral therapy is usually undertaken. If this does not produce the desired effects or does not work at all, the clinician may decide to subject the patient to pharmacological treatment.

Of course, even with regard to pharmacological intervention, you will have to choose the most appropriate ones for your specific case. The therapeutic regimen, in fact, will have to be discussed and decided by mutual agreement between the doctor and the patient, in this case, you.

Medication issues, in fact, are often more complicated for women with ADHD than for men. Any pharmacological approach must take into consideration all aspects of the woman's life, which are not only relational. Particular attention, in fact, must be paid to biological hormonal conditions, menstrual cycle, pregnancy, and menopause, with an increase in ADHD symptoms whenever estrogen levels decrease.

What does drug therapy consist of in adult woman with ADHD?

Well, now that we know that it is essential to consult a psychiatrist or neurologist, know that the main thing to know is both the risks and benefits of the medications you are going to take. In general, the therapy might be similar to that administered for children, but obviously the dosage is different, as are the hormonal fluctuations. To better understand how ADHD might affect your life based on hormonal cycles, we refer you to reading the first manual. Anyway, drug therapy in the adult woman (or adults in general) for the treatment of ADHD symptoms involves the administration of:

1. Stimulant drugs based on methylphenidate or amphetamines increase and balance chemicals in the brain. Treatment with stimulants has positive effects on the most disabling symptoms and behaviors of ADHD in adult women. In addition to trying to dampen the most disabling aspects of the disorder, treatment with these stimulant medications also goes a long way in improving other related aspects such as low self-esteem, anger

episodes, mood swings, cognitive problems and family relationships. The dose of medication to be taken is always determined by the doctor on an individual basis. In any case, it is necessary not to exceed the maximum dose of 60 mg of methylphenidate per day. Depending on the pharmaceutical form used, the drug can be taken as a single dose, or in split doses throughout the day.
2. Non-stimulant medication such as atomoxetine and some antidepressants such as bupropion. Non-stimulant medication treatments involving atomoxetine may be indicated especially in those adult patients with comorbid substance abuse disorders, emotional disorders, or anxiety and social phobia (to learn more about comorbidity go review the specific section in the first manual). The dose of atomoxetine usually used in adults is 80-100 mg per day. These types of non-stimulant medications act much slower than stimulant medications but could be good alternatives if you cannot take stimulants due to specific health issues. Or in the case of certain hormonal phases in a woman's life.

Of course, both of these types of medications can cause side effects in adults.
Regarding stimulant drugs, the most commonly reported adverse effects include stomach upset such as nausea, vomiting, headache, lack of appetite, insomnia, and xerostomia. Regarding non-stimulant drugs, the most manifest side effects include nausea, vomiting, constipation, dry mouth, dizziness, drowsiness or insomnia, loss of sex drive, weight loss, and lack of appetite.

Alternative to drugs: Homeopathy and Phytotherapy

After reviewing useful medications for treating ADHD, we wonder if there are homeopathic and herbal remedies for ADHD.
Before talking about these possible remedies, we remind you that it is always useful to take a conscious approach to the care of your

own health. Therefore, before looking for alternatives, it is always useful to consult your trusted doctor.

It is important to consider how knowledge not verified by scientifically recognized clinical studies should always be evaluated with extreme caution. It is still a field that differs completely from traditional medicine. These remedies, in fact, can be counted among unconventional medicines.

And it is well known that unconventional medicine has the tendency to seek a holistic approach towards the disease, considering "the sick" in its complexity of individual and wholeness, beyond the single diseased organ. This vision allows this type of non-conventional medicine to be able to intervene on multiple levels and above all through different and complementary "paths", even apparently "distant" from the disease as a pure nosological entity.

Homeopathy for ADHD

According to homeopathy, disease in general can be defined as an attempt by our organism to restore the general balance. General balance that for some cause has been lost. What homeopathy does, therefore, is to establish what may be the best remedies based on the overall assessment of the symptoms of the organism as a whole (as we said above the so-called holistic approach).

Specifically, homeopathic remedies that can be used to treat attention deficit hyperactivity disorder (ADHD) are identified from the symptoms presented by the patient and their prevalence and incidence. The most common remedies include regarding ADHD and homeopathy might be:

- Agaricus Muscaricus
- Anacardium
- Carbon Bar
- Carbonic Limestone
- Sulfuric Limestone
- Carcinosinum
- China
- Hyoscyamus
- Kali Bromatum

- Lac Panicum
- Lycopodium
- Medorrhinum
- Mercurius Solubilis
- Sulfur
- Stramonium

Phytotherapy and ADHD

Phytotherapy is, probably unlike homeopathy, much closer to classical pharmacology, which was also born with the study of medicinal plants and compounds present in them. It is right to remind you as the same World Health Organization has established guidelines for the evaluation of the efficacy and safety of medicinal plants.

Phytotherapy, as the term itself, says, employs the use of plants for curative purposes. The plant can be used entirely, but more frequently you can select the parts (leaves, roots, stem, fruits) that have a higher concentration of active ingredients responsible for pharmacological activity such as, for example, essential oils, flavonoids, alkaloids, etc..

, specifically, the phytotherapeutic approach to treating ADHD, will go after the root cause to alleviate the symptoms. We reiterate, however, that any treatment for ADHD will never be directed at eliminating the underlying cause of the disorder, but only at alleviating the more severe manifestations of the disorder. In any case, the phytotherapeutic approach for ADHD will focus on the use of herbal drugs that can promote the elimination of heavy metals from the body, which are believed to be the possible cause of the disorder, as well as remedies with tonic effects on the central nervous system and/or mild hypnotic and sedative effects.

In herbal medicine, medicinal plants for ADHD might include:
- Avena sativa (Oat)
- Coriandrum (Coriander)
- Fucus Versicolor (Fucus)
- Humulus lupulus (Hop)
- Matricaria camomilla (Chamomile)

- Nepeta cataria (Catnip)
- Primula veris (Primrose)
- Scutellaria laterifolia (Scutellaria)
- European Tilia (Common Lime)
- Trifolium pratense (Clover)
- Urtica dioica (Nettle)
- Verbena officinalis (Vervain)

We reiterate, with regard to both homeopathy and phytotherapy, that these are not, however, approved and official therapies, and for this reason, we again advise you to evaluate alternative treatments with your clinician.

Psychoeducation for the adult woman with ADHD

As we have said many times, therapy for ADHD must be based on a multimodal approach that succeeds in combining psychoeducational interventions with drug therapy in cases of ADHD.

The first approach that is used and therefore takes priority over pharmacological treatment is psychoeducation. The adult woman with ADHD, or an adult, diagnosed with ADHD should be informed about the effects of the disorder and how psychological treatment can actively act on these effects. An important piece, therefore, of the modal approach to treating ADHD in the adult woman involves, first of all, the development of individualized knowledge and awareness of the consequences that ADHD has on one's life, day to day.

How does psychological treatment work in adult woman with ADHD?

After explaining the importance and first of psychoeducation and psychotherapy in the treatment of adult women with ADHD, let's look at how these methods work specifically.

Educating the patient (in this case the adult woman but also those close to her) allows for a better understanding of the symptoms and associated disability, brain dysfunction and the risk of developing other disorders. This type of treatment favors better management of the difficulties related to the pathology, also making the family members more aware. It also makes them more supportive of a disorder that is so disabling to a woman's life.

Regardless, both psychoeducation and psychotherapy could produce the following results:

- Of optimizing organization and time management.
- Of improving overall organizational skills.
- To learn how to better manage impulsive behaviors.
- To develop problem-solving skills.
- Of improvement in coping with social and work failures.
- To increase their self-esteem and self-perception.
- Of learning ways to improve relationships with family, colleagues, and friends.
- To learn strategies to control one's temperament and the most disabling episodes.

Psychosocial treatment in the adult woman with ADHD

Although ADHD is a neurobiological disorder, we pointed out in the first manual that, especially in the case of adults, it carries with it other disorders in comorbidity such as depressed mood, anxiety, or substance and alcohol abuse. As we said above, while medication can indeed improve ADHD symptomatology, in reality many people continue to experience problems modifying dysfunctional behavioral patterns learned in the past. We know that ADHD already begins in childhood with dysfunctional behaviors. These erroneous behavior patterns still carry over into adulthood, especially the most disabling ones, such as those related to procrastination and poor time and money management skills. It is women, in particular, who reflect these dysfunctional behaviors. At this point, it may well come into play, cognitive behavioral therapy (CBT). This type of therapy stands as a really critical piece of multimodal treatment for people with ADHD, along with counseling and psychoeducation meetings. This is also where affection comes into play: in addition to these meetings, couple or family therapy sessions are useful for adult woman with ADHD. These meetings, in fact, can be useful in improving interpersonal communication and reducing conflict. Already in the first manual, we noted that couples meetings, especially in the sexual sphere, can be decisive in alleviating all those problems that arise during intimacy.

Also speaking of the relational and personal realm, ADHD-focused therapies have been increasingly developed recently to address a wide range of issues, including self-esteem, interpersonal and family problems, daily habits, daily stress levels, and coping skills to adapt to issues related to the disorder. These types of therapies consist of interventions that are often referred to as" neurocognitive psychotherapy." These interventions focus primarily on the life management skills of the adult woman with ADHD to improve cognitive functions (remembering, reasoning, understanding, problem-solving, evaluating and using judgment); but they are also quite functional in learning compensatory strategies and restructuring the environment, both domestic and professional.

Anyway, in summary, these more innovative interventions include:

- ✓ Cognitive-behavioral therapy: this is specifically directed at behavior management and restructuring of dysfunctional negative thoughts. In this way, it is possible for the woman suffering from ADHD to cope with daily tasks in various contexts of life such as family, work or interpersonal relationships. Psychotherapy also provides support for depression, anxiety states and substance abuse disorder.
- ✓ Family support: the participation of family members is also very important in the psychosocial treatment phase of adult women with ADHD. In fact, the support of family members serves to ensure that ADHD women can better cope with their symptoms on the one hand, while on the other hand it is possible for family members (and partners in particular) to bear

the stress of living with an ADHD subject and learn how to help him/her.

These were the primary therapies for treating women with ADHD. In the next section, we will examine alternative approaches to managing the symptoms of this particular disorder.

Alternative approaches for adult women with ADHD

The ones we've shown you above are all possible approaches to multimodal treatment of the disabling effects of ADHD. These are approved treatments and protocols. In this section of the text, we will deal instead with showing you what the alternative approaches are. We speak of alternative and unofficial approaches, precisely because they are hypothetical studies that are not 100% proven and approved, and that need further clinical studies, as well as the consultation of the clinician himself on the possibility of an alternative to the official protocol. There are, therefore, authors who have hypothesized that, given the high comorbidity between Borderline Personality Disorder and ADHD, and the common symptoms (such as impulsivity, emotional dysregulation, substance abuse, low self-esteem, and difficulties in interpersonal relationships), personalized skills training treatment is needed. Personalized refers to treatment that is adapted and shaped based on the specific symptomatology of ADHD in the adult woman. Hypotheses are also related to the possible benefits that these skills may offer to adult patients with ADHD. In this regard, a pilot study, with a small sample and no control group, was conducted to test this hypothesis.

In this study, a protocol was studied and proposed in 13 group sessions, of weekly frequency, lasting two hours each. What was proposed is:
- Clarification: having a psychoeducational approach to the disorder and comparison by each participant of the diagnostic criteria with their own experience.

- Neurobiology/Mindfulness I: psychoeducation on the neurobiological nature of the attentional disorder and the first part of DBT mindfulness training.
- Mindfulness II: DBT mindfulness training. Three 'what' skills: observe, describe and participate; three 'how' skills: non-judgmental perspective, focus on one element at a time, and effectiveness.
- Chaos and Control: presentation of time planning and organization techniques, and discussion of them in daily life.
- Dysfunctional Behaviors/Behavioral Analysis I: definition of dysfunctional behaviors that patients want to change, behavior analysis, and strategies for change.
- Behavior analysis II: behavior analysis and change strategies.
- Emotional regulation: psychoeducation related to emotions, emotional analysis exercises, and regulation exercises in accordance with the principles of DBT.
- Depression/Therapy in ADHD: psychoeducation on typical depressive states secondary to the disorder and coping strategies.
- Impulse control: behavioral analysis (especially regarding anger), short- and long-term negative consequences, and goal-oriented behaviors in accordance with DBT.
- Stress management and more negative emotions: psychoeducation about stress related to one's own performance (both professional and relational), stress management techniques in accordance with patients' resources, and stress tolerance exercises in accordance with DBT.
- Addiction: psychoeducation on the symptoms of alcohol or drug addiction and negative consequences of risky behaviors; behavioral analysis with the development of alternative behavioral strategies.
- ADHD in Relationships/Self-Respect: discussion of the patient's story for interpersonal difficulties encountered and involvement of partners and family members in sharing outside of the group.
- Looking back/forecasting: planning self-help groups and aids.

This treatment protocol showed an improvement in executive functions on the part of adults with ADHD. The downside, however, is that no general improvement in symptomatology was noted; perhaps the most interesting finding is that there were no drop outs or inappropriate behaviors during the course, thus underscoring the effectiveness of the treatment within the therapeutic group.

Other CBT protocols

In addition to this non-productive study of results at the level of symptomatology, subsequently, CBT protocols have been proposed for the treatment of ADHD disorder. Some of these studies are rather dubious in nature. For this reason, we will only show you Safren's protocol (designed and proven in 2010). This choice is simply due to the fact that, as far as the other non-approved protocols are concerned, the authors of these protocols have proposed a 'metacognitive' intervention rather than a real psycho-socio-educational treatment. What we are specifically interested in, in fact, is cognitive behavioral therapy.

Cognitive Behavioral Therapy

Cognitive-behavioral psychotherapy (as we indicated above, CBT) has only recently been considered an additional and effective treatment for ADHD in adults. In our case, that is, in the adult woman, it has in fact been widely demonstrated to be most effective when placed within a multimodal treatment package. In this multimodal treatment that, as we have already seen, includes many pieces, it is, therefore, possible to also include these behavioral interventions aimed at learning and practicing compensatory skills. These interventions work in conjunction with cognitive interventions to treat thinking distortions and the resulting negative emotions that contribute to procrastination and avoidance of certain tasks. It must be said that, in addition to these interventions, the association of possible drug therapy should always be carefully considered especially with regard to the nuclear symptoms of ADHD. In fact, while CBT has a rather limited impact on the nuclear symptoms of ADHD, there is preliminary evidence that it has been shown to be effective on emotional dysregulation. This approach may work more for adults, rather than in children or adolescents, as most of them turn out to be unable to effectively cope with their difficulties and consequently fail to meet the demands of life. In women, specifically, it can act as a regulator of all those negative emotions derived from frustration and failure. But it can also prove useful in removing those negative emotions arising from the onset of anxiety and depression, as well as low self-esteem and self-efficacy.

To get into the details of this type of therapy, we can point you to the main targets:

- ✓ An initial target is where you gain a greater understanding and modification of cognitive biases.
- ✓ A target in which general dysfunctional behavior modification is expected.
- ✓ A target in which you gain better management of mood, anxiety and low self-esteem issues.

The therapeutic strategies that will be used instead are as follows:

- ✓ Cognitive type strategies: these are restructuring strategies, problem-solving organization, time management, procrastination management, psychoeducation, anger management, relationship management, verbal self-instruction, and mindfulness (for strategies on mindfulness, we refer you to the next sections of the text).
- ✓ Emotional: emotion regulation and management, impulse control/self-regulation, self-motivation, increased self-esteem.

Other interventions for the adult woman with ADHD

In addition to multimodal treatment with the various pieces outlined above and alternative interventions such as CBT, ADHD women can benefit from several interventions. Let's take a look below specifically at what these are.

Parent training

We have already been able to look at what parent training is about in the treatment of a child with ADHD. Now let's look at this intervention from another perspective: from the point of view of the role of the adult woman within the family. In most families, the mother in fact has a role of primary importance: she is responsible for cleaning, tidying and general management of the home environment, but also for organizing all family activities. If we think about it, these are all tasks that definitely require attention, concentration, organization and planning. In these cases, ADHD is debilitating, as it compromises all these skills, making the role of mother much more arduous and full of pitfalls than women without this type of disorder. In this case, parent training, given the strong genetic component and correlation of the disorder, can be a greater daily challenge if the ADHD woman is joined by a child with the same disorder. In just such a situation, parent training will provide for a doubling of program integration. On the one hand, in fact, the program will be aimed at managing the behavior of the ADHD child with targeted training; on the other hand, it will meet the mother's needs by reinforcing parenting skills and simplifying activities for the management of the home environment. This type of intervention, therefore, could prove doubly useful and resolve, at least in part, the problems that could arise in a family environment where there are multiple cases of ADHD.

Interventions with support groups

 The problems of ADHD women emerge early and seem to increase in parallel with increasing age. This occurs precisely because of the pressing and ever-increasing demands linked to the social role that women play today, in which they are called upon to manage various activities and situations, all at the same time. In this case, ADHD women generally have lower self-esteem than men with the same disorder, and it is for this very reason that support groups can prove to be crucial and a source of salvation for women with ADHD. Support groups also serve to often overcome a feeling of shame and failure that women with ADHD disorder often experience, especially when compared to non-ADHD women. Group meetings, then, can provide a therapeutic experience, providing a place where the ADHD woman can feel understood and accepted by other women, while at the same time learning to better manage her own life. Also a group in which to feel safe from family, social, and work pressures.

ADHD Coaching

Another alternative method that may prove effective in helping women with ADHD is coaching. Coaching for ADHD essentially allows for the ability to identify the most disabling conditions and daily challenges for the ADHD woman. In addition to allowing these negative challenges and conditions to be identified, a coaching course also allows for the ability to work on emotional and relationship issues. Not only that, it could also prove to be very useful in helping adult women with ADHD to resolve various work and professional conflicts. By identifying the sources of stress in their daily lives, ADHD women will be able to learn useful strategies for dealing with them and manage even the most negative emotions more effectively, thus lowering their stress levels. Always thanks to a coaching course, women with ADHD can also improve their lifestyle, learning to plan moments dedicated to self-care without having to feel guilty. By carving out these moments for herself, the woman with ADHD will be able to relax by engaging in activities that are pleasurable and would bring her greater self-confidence. These could be the activities neglected until the moment of awareness achieved through coaching, precisely because of the previous state of overwhelm and disorganization.

Coaching, therefore, will be focused on the following goals:
- ✓ A formation of a self-image certainly more positive and effective; at the same time the goal is to reduce thoughts related to guilt, failure and inferiority.
- ✓ A reorganization of all daily activities in order of priority, optimizing the time and resources available.

- ✓ Learning techniques for reducing and managing stress and negative emotions.
- ✓ Conflict Management.
- ✓ Acquisition of increased ability to organize, plan and divide work.
- ✓ Increased awareness of one's needs, greater self-care, and adoption of a healthier, more balanced lifestyle.
- ✓ Learning constructive communication skills that allow you to understand the views of others and have your own understanding without misunderstanding.

Alternative tools for the adult with ADHD.

After pointing out all the possible treatments, both approved and alternative ones, let's talk about some tools that can be really helpful in managing ADHD the adult in general. Some researchers believe that adults with this type of disorder have difficulty especially in performing complex tasks. All this is due precisely to the absence of motivation as they are seen by the adult as non-urgent tasks or low emotional component and attractiveness. And therefore we tend to procrastinate. In the last part of the text, there will be a mini-guide on how best to manage time. Here we simply tell you that an alternative solution to such a view could be to use timers so as to generate in the
subject to a perception of speed, of the need to hurry.

In contrast, other authors argue that an effective method of treating ADHD symptoms is to generate contingencies. By creating contingencies, the subject should schedule all of the day's commitments by setting deadlines and departure times to accomplish the task. When generating contingencies, the important thing is to finish the tasks at the scheduled times. For example, when a subject with ADHD has to study a book, he/she may decide that he/she has to prepare 20 pages in 60 minutes, defining the start time and when he/she will have to finish.

Another challenge is distractions that may cause you to overachieve. The first thing you need to do to overcome the distraction factor is to realize that your attention is waning. The first thing to do to overcome the distraction factor is to notice it early enough. However, unproductivity is not so easy to detect, so it is best to seek the help of a therapist, especially when these situations are repeated often and are quite disabling.

Conclusions on therapies for the adult woman with ADHD

In summing up the analyses done on the various treatments for women with ADHD, we can come to some conclusions. One of these is that pharmacological treatment is undoubtedly fundamental in working on the nuclear symptoms of ADHD. Again, according to the analyses carried out, the most studied and most effective pharmacological treatment is that based on stimulants (such as methylphenidate and dexamphetamine). It has been proven that treatment with stimulants has positive effects on both symptoms and behaviors, even the most disabling of ADHD. In adult women, depending on hormonal phases, it also improves other related aspects such as low self-esteem, anger outbursts, mood swings, cognitive problems and family relationships. Non-stimulant therapeutic drug treatments include atomoxetine, which may be indicated for those patients with comorbid substance abuse disorders, emotional disorders or social phobia or anxiety. But these therapies, especially non-stimulant therapies, are not always effective.

Although the efficacy of stimulants in the treatment of ADHD in adults is recognized, their role is still controversial and studied. And as we have previously reiterated, pharmacological treatment does not represent and is not a unique or even priority choice.

Another conclusion is that in addition to pharmacological treatment, psychoeducation should also be added, which represents an important element in the treatment of ADHD in adults, as it allows the patient to be educated to avoid dysfunctional behaviors. And that's not all: thanks to this type of therapy, in addition to the adult woman with ADHD, it is also possible to educate a possible partner and his or her family about the symptoms and disability of ADHD, the prevalence in children and adults, the possibility of comorbidity, heredity, the brain dysfunctions involved and the possibilities of treatment. Providing the patient and her loved ones with all of this information can be of vital help in gaining a deeper understanding of the condition of a woman with ADHD and helping her to cope with the difficulties and problems caused by the disorder. Psychoeducation, in fact, can prove to be a lifeline, in that it produces good effects, even on family relationships, in that this information is shared among family members, and they too become aware of and are able to give an explanation for the patient's behaviors and symptoms.

Finally, it is also necessary to encourage the adult woman with ADHD toward a course of cognitive-behavioral psychotherapy, as patients develop additional issues as a result of the disorder (negative beliefs, low self-esteem, avoidance behaviors, and mood disorders) and in addition, there is a high degree of comorbidity with anxiety disorders, mood disorders, impulse control, and substance abuse.

In essence, the combination of these activities put together can all prove to be key components of an optimal pathway for the management of ADHD and its attendant issues by adult women.

This concludes our overall look at possible therapies for ADHD. In the next section of the text, we will pick up and address in even greater depth the intense emotions that this disorder can involve. Most importantly, we will talk about how to control them through practical tips. This part will then close with a vademecum on how to manage especially anxiety with this disorder.

Part three- how to manage emotions in women with ADHD

Chapter 8: Emotional dysregulation for the adult woman with ADHD.

Moods and emotions for the adult woman with ADHD

Usually, in the adult stage, the symptoms of ADHD are much less visible and recognizable, compared to those that occur primarily in children under the age of 12.

Adult women, in particular, who suffer from this disorder often have to disarm and have conflicting states of mind. In fact, in most cases, women with this disorder experience strong states of anxiety or depression, restlessness, excessive impulsivity, and difficulty paying or maintaining attention to what they are doing.

The consequence of all these symptoms leads to poor judgment, low self-esteem, procrastination to infinity tasks to be completed, continuous and sudden mood swings, serious problems at work, or study and especially in family relationships and emotional.

Emotional and emotional issues, especially in women who suffer from ADHD are often the ones that are not taken into consideration, but they are the ones that cause most of the problems for those who suffer from this disorder.

In fact, Dr. Thomas Brown, in the course of his research on ADHD, has shown that the cause of sudden outbursts of anger and excessive frustration in ADHD sufferers are not given due consideration, simply because the diagnostic criteria for ADHD do not evaluate emotional disturbances as being part of the symptoms of the disorder, causing many therapists to not adequately assess the actual impact they have on the person.

However, also thanks to his studies, it has been widely demonstrated that people who suffer from ADHD, and in our specific case women who suffer from this disorder, have much more difficulty in managing their emotions. Difficulties that are greater even than those who, while not suffering from ADHD, have problems in themselves managing anger, impulsivity, stress, anxiety and depression.

It has also been shown, from the different studies carried out, that about 33% of people with ADHD, suffer from disorders of the emotional sphere, stating that for them this is the most degrading and harmful condition of the whole disease.

So women who suffer from this disorder, in addition to dealing with the typical symptoms of the disease, often face increasing challenges and symptoms.

In the next few paragraphs we will consider the various emotional states that involve women suffering from ADHD, you will also be advised on how to cope with these emotions, especially one of the disorders involving the emotional sphere will be considered, which is related to anxiety disorder. Being able to better understand and manage these feelings will help you alleviate them and alleviate the guilt and sense of confusion that often affects women suffering from ADHD.

Emotional dysregulation in those with ADHD

Emotional dysregulation is another essential component of ADHD symptomatology, and if it were given due consideration during the diagnosis of the disorder, neither would certainly allow for a more effective understanding.

Although it is unclear what the connection is between the two syndromes, it has been found that about 40% of people who suffer from ADHD suffer from emotional dysregulation at the same time.

In fact, several studies conducted recently have shown that emotional dysregulation is a symptom that was previously ignored among the criteria for diagnosis, since it was included as a temperamental deficit or as a consequence of a deficit in executive functions and therefore as a dysfunction in the inhibition of behavioral control, physiological states and refocusing of attention. At the theoretical level, according to the first hypothesis, emotional dysregulation is seen as a mental process that is totally dissociated from the quintessential emotional experience.

In addition, depending on which subtype of ADHD one suffers from, emotional regulation occurs differently, which is classified according to the dimensions of temperament. According to this approach, it turns out that negative and positive emotionality are two dimensions that are totally independent of cognitive control.

The second hypothesis, sees emotional dysregulation as a consequence of a deficit in executive functions. In this second hypothesis, temperamental elements are not taken into account but emotional control is under cognitive control.

Starting from this second hypothesis, other research has been carried out where it has been hypothesized that emotional dysregulation in ADHD can be considered as "deficient emotional self-regulation" (DESR). By this we refer in particular to:

- Difficulty inhibiting inappropriate behaviors in response to negative feelings and emotions.
- Difficulty maintaining attention following strong emotions, whether positive or negative.
- Disorganization of behavior as a result of the emotional response.
- A deficit in the organization of arousal (is a temporary condition of the central nervous system, which is triggered following a significant stimulus of varying intensity or a general state of arousal. This condition is characterized by an increased attentional-cognitive state of alertness and prompt reaction to external stimuli) following a strong emotional response.

What is also emphasized by the researchers is that emotional dysregulation must be distinguished and differentiated from other disorders of the neurological sphere such as for example depression, anxiety, or bipolar disorder.

Recent studies on emotional dysregulation and ADHD have highlighted how poor emotional regulation in those suffering from this disorder, affects the mechanisms that regulate and inhibit the dominant automatic response to a stimulus, voluntarily modifying both attention and behavior.

So, from all the research that has been done, it turns out that, in ADHD sufferers, emotional dysregulation causes abrupt changes in behavior and mood and in the ability to handle emotionally derived situations that can be triggered either by a single event or by a distressing situation that is still ongoing. So basically, an emotional breakdown is just what it sounds like, the inability to manage, compose, or contextualize an emotion.

All this leads to practical problems during the management of their lives, such as abruptly interrupting an interpersonal relationship, which is love or friendship, having great problems managingsitively negative situations, until they get to real serious mental illnesses such as anxiety disorders or depression.

This is why it is important to include cognitive-behavioral therapy in the management of ADHD, as it is one of the best therapies that give real support in dealing with and managing emotions. Thanks to this type of therapy you will be able to perceive on a conscious level the emotions that cause you state of stress, minimizing frustration and self-criticism and becoming aware of the behavioral patterns that often lead to these states of emotional distress.

What are the typical characteristics of emotional dysregulation

As we saw in the previous section, emotional dysregulation is a consequence of poor executive function control in those with ADHD. This leads to the following consequences:
- Impatience and a low tolerance for frustrating events.
- Excessive outbursts of anger.
- Continuous mood swings are much more amplified than normal.

- Problems in regulating emotional states lead to very intense and overwhelming emotional reactions.
- Difficulty inhibiting behavioral responses to emotion and difficulty moderating the intensity of this emotional response.
- Difficulty refocusing attention after intense emotional discharge.
- Difficulty in organizing and giving appropriate responses, due to the lack of flexibility in the cognitive area responsible for manipulating and organizing information.

The consequences of these deficits caused by emotional dysregulation are:

- Experience, feel, express and undergo emotions in a stronger and more intense way, especially in the sentimental sphere.
- Becoming overly excited and restless.
- Focus solely and exclusively on the negative aspects of life.
- Being the victim of a variety of problems at the social and work levels, such as bullying, rejection, and isolation both socially and emotionally, such as relationship breakdown, divorce or marital problems.
- Having difficulties in school or work, such as problems finding a job, always being the focus of disciplinary measures, lack of promotions or bonuses the constant loss of any kind of work or activity you decide to undertake.
- Constant anxiety about strong emotions often leads to depressive states or anxiety disorders.
- Being involved in illegal and criminal activities.

Chapter 9: Emotion management for the woman with ADHD.

What anxiety disorder in women with ADHD consists of

People who suffer from ADHD, as we have said, in addition to the typical symptoms that are inattention, hyperactivity and impulsivity, develop at early age disorders in the purely psychological sphere, such as sleep disorders.

Most notably, however, a distressing and socially debilitating feeling develops is an anxiety disorder.

Between 25% and 40% of adults with ADHD also have anxiety disorders. Among these, more than half are the female adult population with ADHD. In addition, anxiety disorder is perceived more strongly and intensely in women with ADHD.

Anxiety disorder, in person suffering from this disorder, can manifest itself in different ways, such as mood swings, difficulties at the cognitive level or the behavioral level, to real physical problems. The common characteristics of anxiety disorder are excessive fear, nervousness and worries about facts and events of no importance. All this is then also accompanied by a strong state of physical and emotional restlessness, being always alarmed, strong concentration problems, sleep disorders, perennial states of irritability, feelings of overwhelm, but also to stiffness at the musculoskeletal level, and fatigue both physical and emotional.

Very often, women who suffer from an anxiety disorder often have a feeling that leads even to terror, of being spied on or always being judged by the people around them. Thus leading them to destroy the low self-esteem they already have because of ADHD.

As it is easy to understand, for a woman who has these strong feelings completely invalidating it is really difficult to relax or manage her life and her social and emotional sphere.

Women who suffer from ADHD-related anxiety states will then begin to prefer isolation so that they can avoid all situations that, in their view, could only lead to a negative outcome.

In addition, the anxiety disorder only worsens the procrastination process typical of ADHD sufferers, or it may exacerbate decision-making or the need to repeatedly find reassurance to one's concerns, which are usually the cause of the failure of ADHD sufferers' relationships.

How to combat anxiety disorder if you have ADHD

As we have seen, it is very simple that typical ADHD symptoms easily overlap and intertwine with anxiety disorder symptoms.

The first step you'll need to take to solve this terrible problem is to figure out if this deficit comes from and is inextricably linked with ADHD or if it is the result of an anxiety disorder entirely separate from this issue.

Anxiety, in fact, may occur regardless of whether you have ADHD, or it may already be present as a comorbid state, or be a direct consequence of ADHD.

For example, an anxiety disorder may result from a side effect of medications used to treat ADHD.

Usually the comorbidity symptoms are:
- Difficulty socializing.
- Agitation.
- Difficulty with concentration and attention.
- Difficulty completing an assigned task.
- Excessive irritability.

In terms of differences, the main ones between the two syndromes are as follows:
- Anxiety disorder primarily causes symptoms such as agitation, worry, or fear. ADHD is primarily characterized by a lack of attention and agitation.

- Anxiety disorder often leads to compulsive behavior or extremely perfectionistic behavior, which is completely absent in people with ADHD.

To treat anxiety disorder, many treating physicians resort to drug therapy. However, very often, the medications are used only to make the situation worse, so choosing an alternative route would, in fact, be the best situation. Although, in fact, drug therapy is the one of choice to treat both symptoms, very often it is not the ideal solution for everyone.

Cognitive behavioral therapy to combat anxiety disorder

Cognitive-behavioral therapy is a particular type of psychological therapy, short-term, which manages to help patients to change their patterns and mental schemes, to influence, in a positive way, the behavior of patients themselves. Usually, this is the therapy used to treat anxiety disorders in a non-pharmacological way and it has also proved to be excellent for those who have associated ADHD as a disorder.

Relaxation techniques to combat anxiety disorder

This category includes all types of relaxation, whether psychological, autogenic training, progressive muscle relaxation, visualization techniques, meditation, or deep breathing. Basically, all those relaxation techniques that cure stress and anxiety by slowing the heart rate, reducing muscle tension and increasing concentration are good.

Some tips to be able to manage anxiety at the best

Anxiety disorder, associated with ADHD needs to be, first and foremost, followed by a professional. Traditional treatment, in fact, involves the combined use of medication and psychological therapy.

However, there are steps you can take, coupled with the right therapy for you, to alleviate and counteract the symptoms. In fact, people who suffer from ADHD can easily manage both conditions if they learn to take certain steps and changes in their lifestyle.

- Try to understand what triggers the disorder. Many times, this disorder, is caused by specific causes or particular events. Once you have identified what, specifically, the triggers are, talk to your therapist so that you can come up with a solution on how best to handle these situations.
- Try to get enough sleep. The advice is to get at least 7 hours of sleep per night. Poor sleep quality and the resulting stress very often exacerbate the anxiety disorder. Since, with ADHD, it is often difficult to sleep properly and in a period of time that is conducive to mental and physical well-being, meditation and relaxation techniques can help. Very often, medications that are prescribed for both anxiety and ADHD interfere with good-quality sleep. In this case, try to find a solution with your doctor, especially if you also plan to take something supplemental to help you sleep.
- Keep a planner for all of your commitments. When you have ADHD, it is very difficult to get a task done. This very often triggers the anxiety disorder that is associated with ADHD. Keeping a journal with a detailed schedule of everything you need to do will help you not only to complete the task but also to fade away the anxiety states associated with failure.
- Dedicate yourself to physical activity. Moving outdoors or practicing any kind of sport is very useful to counteract anxiety disorder. This is because, in addition to the gradual release of dopamine, during exercise you always tend to release stress

and tension that very often cause anxiety. Exercise is also a very useful and healthy way to break the daily routine related to work or family and to be able to recharge the mind and body from the fatigue accumulated during the performance of these activities.
- Start minimizing events. Whatever the cause that triggers your anxiety disorder, starting to minimize and view in a positive way even events that seem to be catastrophic will greatly help you manage your anxiety. Therefore, start accepting in a positive way not only the pessimistic thoughts that hover in your mind but also the actual situations that happen to you in life. Seeing positively the negative aspects will help you to fight especially the fear of others and the fear of failure, also increasing your self-esteem.
- Don't demand too much of yourself. One of the problems related to ADHD and which often generates states of anxiety are the enormous expectations that are very often above anyone's real possibilities. So start by setting realistic and easily achievable goals for yourself. Learning to understand what your limits are and accept when it's time to say enough, will help you not only to get to the point of not being able to do it anymore, but it will significantly reduce the stress levels that cause your annoying states of anxiety. So devote yourself to projects that are sustainable for you and you will begin to experience fewer of the panic attacks typical of anxiety disorder.

Practical tips on how to manage emotions

As we have seen ADHD can trigger a number of conflicting emotional emotions. Many of these emotions trigger reactions that are very often negative, such as feeling perpetually judged or feeling guilty for not meeting your expectations or those of others. Many times you also feel stressed and guilty because those around you are unlikely to understand that your lack of stimulation and inattention is not of your own making.

Your emotions are similar to those of millions of people, the drawback is, in your case, that because of ADHD, you feel these emotions amplified and lingering for longer than normal.

If you suffer from ADHD, drug treatment and the right therapy can help you greatly in dealing with these negative emotions.

However, there are steps you can take in your daily life to better manage and regulate your emotions. The following is a series of useful tips for dealing with the strong emotions caused by your disorder.

Learn how to manage stress

Generally, any adult woman working or running a home and family will experience physical and emotional states of high stress. Normal levels of stress very often are helpful in keeping you focused on what you are doing or what you need to do.

However, prolonged levels of stress can lead to negative reactions and can lead to pathological states of mind and body such as, for example, depression or cardiovascular problems.

If you suffer from ADHD, in addition to drug therapy, to manage stress you can try meditation and relaxation techniques, typical of sports activities such as yoga.

Also, try to remove from your life not only all stressors but also emotionally damaging people who instead of helping you will only make your situation worse.

Another very useful way to deal with stress is to minimize the extra activities that you have set your mind to follow. If you fail to complete all the tasks that you have set for yourself, leading you to be perpetually under stress, what you need to do is simply remove some of these activities from your list that are not absolutely practical or necessary.

Listen carefully to your thoughts

People who suffer from ADHD often have negative thoughts that plague them at any point in their lives. Some of the most common thoughts include self-pity, self-punishing thoughts, catastrophizing, and brooding.

To learn how to deal with all these negative thoughts, it would be very useful to write a diary, where you take notes, marking what kind of thoughts you are haunted by and how often.

Having done that, you should then write next to the negative thought that haunts you, the opposite, that is, the positive thought opposite to your negative thought. And then, in conclusion, try to keep your attention firmly on the corresponding positive, until, in the end, you manage your emotions to the best of your ability.

Take a break

Once you have identified your stressors, it would be very helpful, to be able to find some time is an appropriate space, to pause your life. During this time, you could try to reflect on everything that causes you stress, anxiety or any other type of negative emotion and find ways to keep your distance from all these devastating states of your disorder. In addition, this space-time all to yourself will also give you a chance to process all the negative emotions and feelings and turn them into positive emotions, situations and feelings.

Learn the art of silence

Learn to put a brake between your thoughts and your language. Basically, you should learn to think more and keep those thoughts to yourself and speak a little less. Also learn to become better listeners, to not constantly interrupt your interlocutors, but to listen to what they are communicating to you. This way you will not only not have any more problems in the social sphere but also in the work sphere.

Find the time and space to be able to give vent to your emotions

In addition to finding space and time to manage your daily stress, you should also find time to give free rein to your negative emotions and feelings. Letting these feelings surface anywhere and at any time can almost certainly not lead to anything good.

One way to better manage your emotions would be to find, at least for an hour a day, physical activities where you will have to use all your energy so that you can discharge anger, stress, tension and also the pain caused by all these negative feelings.

Having done that, also remember that after the outburst, you should find some time to be calm.

Learn to manage mood swings, avoid blame

Once you have begun to understand what stressful situations are causing you to have constant mood swings, you need to focus on overcoming these mood swings rather than remaining fixated on why they may have happened. Also, you should stop looking for a culprit for these situations, whether it is you or others. Rather, spend your time figuring out what strategies to carry out to make the problem resolve itself positively and quickly.

A very helpful way to deal with mood swings would be to engage in some practical activity as soon as you feel completely overwhelmed. For example, you could start reading a book, or look for a friend to strike up a conversation with that has nothing too challenging as its topic, devote yourself to taking care of your garden, or watch an entertaining and relaxing television program.

Remind yourself constantly and repeatedly that this feeling is only passing and that it is better to deal with it than to try to figure it out.

Try to be mentally prepared to deal with bad days

Quite often, someone with ADHD has a particular way of dealing with events and situations compared to a person who does not have this disorder. For example, for a person who suffers from ADHD, a happy, exciting event or success instead of creating positive moods can also lead to having depressive states.

If you are aware that these moods are routine for you, then it would be best to already leave prepared for the sense of depression that accompanies you at the end of each event.

You could, for example, turn to friends and family who are ready to distract you at the exact moment when you know you are feeling these strong negative emotions, or perhaps you can engage in fun and relaxing activities or decide to take up physical activity at the moment when depression starts to set in. In this regard, you can pack your gym bag in advance so that you are ready the instant you need it.

Try to put a sense of humor and positive feelings first

Try not to stay angry or feel guilty for long about your negative emotions. Instead, learn to laugh more often, not only at funny things but also try to laugh and play it down and maybe take yourself a little less seriously. Learn to make light of your mistakes, trying to improve but not to catastrophize events. All this will lead you to have better relationships not only with yourself but especially with others. With this, however, you are not advised to downplay and make light of all kinds of mistakes you make throughout your life. There are mistakes for which you need to take responsibility for your actions. However, for those with ADHD, there are trivial and insignificant mistakes that can create emotional distress, and these are the ones that need to be taken with a smile, and approached lightly so that you can move on safely and not make them again in the future. Furthermore, by pointing out your faults in an ironic way, you will realize that those around you will be willing to accept your mistakes much more easily and with leniency and understanding.

Try to be more kind and helpful to the people around you

When you suffer from ADHD, it is easy to get into a vicious cycle based on self-criticism and compulsive obsession with the small and insignificant things in life. One way to break out of this vicious cycle is to turn your attention away from yourself and try to direct your attention to others.

Of course, for those who suffer from this disorder, it will be a little more complicated to establish an empathetic relationship with those around you, however, with a little practice and perseverance, you will surely succeed in paying more and more attention to the needs of others.

Concentration directed at other people's feelings can not only help you greatly in distracting yourself from your negative feelings but will help you build many stable social relationships.

Avoid medications or substances known to have mood-altering abilities

Regarding drug therapy, the advice is simple: follow only the therapy prescribed by your doctor. Avoid categorically illegal substances or drugs that have not been examined by your doctor.

As for other mood-altering substances, we are referring specifically to alcohol. Try to consume alcohol in moderation, even though it would actually be a good idea to eliminate it completely from your life. Drink, always in excessive moderation, only on special occasions or weekends when you go out with friends, and absolutely avoid drinking on work days.

The use of these substances is deleterious in your case because, in addition to increasing your emotional vulnerability, and making you experience stronger negative feelings, you will not only experience this effect the moment you take these substances, but it could last for days.

Increase things to do or learn on a daily basis

Learning something or doing something is a very enjoyable feeling, as it will give you a sense of confidence and mastery that you are not usually used to feeling. You can for example try to improve your ability to learn your native language or a new language, learn to cook something new every day, learn to do new activities or incorporate new exercises daily into your physical activity will give you more mastery over your emotions, increasing positive feelings such as self-esteem and a sense of belonging and usefulness that is often lacking in those with ADHD.

Try to approach the future in a positive way

By this we don't mean consulting a magician to find out what your future holds, but the advice is to plan. Especially mark in a journal and plan in advance what your response to an intense emotional state might be.

Mark in your journal what particular situations usually trigger a strong and intense emotional response in you, and then also mark what you need and how best to deal with these situations. In this way you will be prepared to deal positively with the negative situation that comes your way.

The advice, moreover, is not to get discouraged if on the first attempt this technique does not give the results you hope for. Many times it is necessary to test several alternatives before finding the one that works best in your specific case. Another very useful tip, to make the strategies you are going to use work best, is to try them not only in moments of strong agitation but especially when you are in a state of calm.

This concludes our practical part on managing emotions. In the next, even more, practical part, we will delve into the topic of nutrition and correct lifestyles for managing ADHD. Guidance will be given, therefore, on how to eat and what are the correct eating habits for those with ADHD. In addition to healthy eating, there will be guidance on sleep habits and how sports can help.

Part four: proper nutrition and lifestyle to be able to manage ADHD

Chapter 10: Ideal Nutrition for a Woman with ADHD

In addition to drug and psychiatric therapy, lifestyle changes must be made, particularly in the developmental years, to achieve optimal results in the management of ADHD.

Starting first of all with play. Improving this aspect implies bringing children to play outdoors, doing a lot of movement and physical activity that is fun and stimulating, running and playing, but all in a healthy and controlled way, to improve not only the quality of life but also the social aspect of the child suffering from ADHD.

In addition to this, a healthy and correct diet must also be added. Many studies, conducted on preadolescent children, have shown the exacerbation of symptoms, especially the symptoms of hyperkinesis, due to a completely wrong diet, based mainly on refined sugars, colorings and sweeteners, chemical additives, and preservatives. All of these elements negatively affect both the emotions and behaviors of those with ADHD.

The importance of a healthy and proper diet in those with ADHD

An unhealthy and unbalanced diet consisting only of foods lacking essential nutrients and containing only industrially sourced ingredients is detrimental to anyone's health.

The nutrition conversation is even more important if you have ADHD. Decreasing, if not eliminating, foods containing harmful substances, such as artificial dyes and preservatives, can both improve symptoms on a behavioral level and provide tremendous health benefits.

In addition, as studies conducted by Dr. Anna Esparham of the Department of Pediatrics at the University of Kansas Medical Center have shown, a healthy diet, especially when eaten as a child and continued throughout adolescence, is essential for promoting long-term nervous system function.

Consulting a nutrition expert is one of the best approaches to understanding and correcting poor eating behaviors from an early age, which, while it is true that they do not cause ADHD, are certainly responsible for exacerbating many of the symptoms of this disorder.

In fact, while many foods are harmful to those suffering from ADHD, there are other foods that are very useful for the proper functioning of brain cells and for increasing attention and concentration skills. For example, you should increase your consumption of protein, especially from eggs, nuts, and legumes. The consumption of these foods, in fact, promotes concentration and, consequently, improves learning. The daily consumption of fresh seasonal fruits and vegetables is also necessary. However, the consumption of fruits and vegetables should be moved mainly in the evening hours, as these foods promote physical and mental relaxation, also promoting a good quality of sleep.

As we will see later, in the part about supplementation, it is of vital importance to consume foods containing high quantities of omega-3 fatty acids, which are mainly found in fish such as salmon, tuna, and mackerel and oily fish such as sardines.

That being said, what are the foods that you should definitely avoid if you suffer from this disorder? Below you will be provided with a list of all the substances that are harmful to your well-being and only useful in worsening the symptoms of ADHD.

- Sugar: the sugar contained in many foods and sugary drinks not only provides calories that are completely unnecessary for the body, but can also cause dysfunctions in the brain. In order to improve ADHD symptoms, it would be necessary to reduce sugar consumption to a minimum, if not almost completely abolish it. About 66% of young people who regularly consume sugary or energy drinks suffer from hyperactivity and attention deficit disorder. In any case, the use of artificial sweeteners is also to be discouraged because, according to one study, many people with ADHD who used sugar substitutes very often found themselves having severe migraines, as well as the exacerbation of attention and learning disorders in non-adult subjects. However, a very important fact must be emphasized. While it is true that cutting down on refined sugars helps counteract the symptoms of ADHD, it is not healthy to completely eliminate carbohydrates from your diet. Therefore, the solution is to replace refined carbohydrates with whole-grain ones.

- Food dyes: most of these elements are found in foods that have a long shelf life and in carbonated and sugary drinks. In this case you should totally eliminate from your daily diet any type of product that contains artificial coloring, not only to improve ADHD symptoms but to avoid, on the contrary, that they worsen.
- Gluten-containing foods: much research has shown that this waste product is responsible for exacerbating ADHD symptoms in both children and adults. In fact, during the study, it was shown that the subjects who participated, showed an improvement in symptoms from the first days in which they began to follow a gluten-free diet. For this reason, according to the researchers, it would be necessary to include celiac disease in the list of causes of the disorder. A proper diet requires that you eliminate all foods that contain gluten. Among these are non-whole wheat pasta and bread, products made with overly refined flour and packaged foods.
- Caffeine: A study has shown that, especially about young people suffering from ADHD, consumption of coffee or products containing caffeine, increases angry and violent behaviors. For this reason, both adults and adolescents suffering from ADHD should avoid energy drinks and all products that contain caffeine and other types of stimulants. Even if stimulant-acting drugs are prescribed in the pharmacological treatment for ADHD, stimulant foods and drinks mustn't be included in the diet,

because, unlike drugs, these substances increase anxiety, hyperactivity, aggression and insomnia.
- Monosodium glutamate, yeast extract and hydrolyzed vegetable protein: ADHD sufferers should avoid these foods. The reason they should be eliminated is that these types of food additives significantly decrease dopamine levels. This stimulates negative ADHD symptoms such as impulsivity and hyperactivity.
- Nitrites: most industrial and pre-packaged foods contain these substances. Nitrites cause increased anxiety disorder and restlessness.

What is and what is the specific diet for those suffering from ADHD

The perfect diet for those who suffer from this type of disorder is no different from many the diets, such as the Mediterranean diet, which promote the consumption of healthy and fresh foods, with a reduced amount of sugars of industrial origin and with the total abolition of artificial products.

On an ideal level, a diet suitable for ADHD sufferers should therefore help the brain function and work better. It should also reduce typical symptoms of this disorder such as hyperactivity and lack of concentration. Such a diet should include both certain foods and the intake of dietary supplements.

Dr. Richard Sogn, an expert in ADHD, has concluded from the various research done on this disorder that any food that is supportive of brain function helps combat disorders related to the disorder.

Since it is very difficult to change eating habits easily, the soft approach might be the ideal solution. For example, you can start by eliminating all sweets and sugar-containing foods, especially those of industrial origin, and replace them with organic foods or sweets made at home with low-sugar flour. Gradually move from replacing sweets to completely abolishing them to direct your attention to healthier foods.

It may also be helpful to consume protein foods throughout the day, including at breakfast, so that you can improve concentration and only take in carbohydrates at dinner so that you can also promote sleep.

As for the protein part, you should consume a lot of salmon, which contains a high dose of omega-3, useful to improve concentration and attention, or legumes and eggs, which contain zinc, useful to reduce hyperactivity, impulsivity and irritability.

Other foods that you should consume regularly are walnuts, almonds and hazelnuts. These foods also contain high amounts of omega-3 but also a large amount of magnesium and vitamin E, which are useful for slowing down the deterioration of cognitive function.

As for vegetables, you should consume more green leafy vegetables, especially spinach, which is rich in magnesium.

Among fruits, bananas surely have an important place, as they are rich in mineral salts, especially magnesium and potassium.

The second vegetable superfood that should not be missing from your daily diet is avocado, as it is rich in monounsaturated fats useful not only for lowering blood pressure, but also because it increases cerebral circulation.

Another food that should not be missing from your diet is berries and especially blueberries. These foods contain antioxidants that help protect brain cells from oxidative stress and increase brain function.

Tuna is another food that is very helpful in combating the symptoms of ADHD. Like salmon, tuna is also rich in omega-3s. Adding tuna to your eating routine is a good and healthy habit if you suffer from ADHD.

How to create a personalized ADHD diet

At this point in the guide, so you may be wondering how to go about making a food plan for you or your child with ADHD.

There are basic steps to follow to choose a healthy and proper diet that is suitable for your needs, or those of your child, and that is especially compatible with your overall health.

For this reason, the first step you should take before starting any kind of dietary regimen is to consult your doctor. This is because the doctor who is following you is the most qualified person to evaluate if the changes you are trying to put in place are useful or effective in your specific case. In addition, your primary care physician will provide you with specific tests to determine if these changes may be making your brain situation worse. This way you will know what diet is the safest and most appropriate for you.

You should also have your health care provider help you monitor the changes after undertaking the new eating regimen to make sure of the actual benefits of these changes.

Once you have consulted your doctor and determined what is appropriate for you, you can move on to the next step.

Whatever dietary regimen you decide to follow, the following are helpful tips to follow to make those changes effective:

- The changes that you should undertake should be taken one at a time and followed step by step. This way you will be able to tell if these changes are actually effective or not.
- Keep a food diary, where you should write down all the changes and modifications you have made to your diet. In the notes it would also be useful to mark all the effects, even negative ones that you have noticed during your journey. Your notes should be shown to your doctor every time you go for a checkup.
- Try to consume fewer carbohydrates and more protein. Protein is critical to maintaining a healthy nervous system and is essential in the formation and production of neurotransmitters. Including a protein element in every meal will ensure that you avoid glycemic spikes, which are known to increase hyperactivity.
- Consume more complex carbohydrates and fewer refined carbohydrates. Just like protein, complex carbohydrates lower blood glucose levels. In addition, complex carbohydrates will make you feel full for longer, making sure you avoid constant

snacking containing sugar. Moreover, this type of carbohydrate, will promote sleep by helping you a lot with your sleep disorders.
- Have healthy, balanced meals. Try to have 3 main meals, interspersed with 2 snacks. All 5 meals should include seasonal fruits and vegetables, protein, and omega-3 and omega-6 acids.
- Try not to skip meals. Skipping a meal, especially one of the three main ones, could lead to a sugar crash, prompting you to eat junk food to quell the hunger.

The best supplements and vitamins for those with ADHD

Supplements and vitamins are definitely one of the most widely used alternative remedies for treating ADHD symptoms. Some of these alternative methods are simpler to find and much cheaper than medications. However, it should be pointed out that these, without the help of drug and psychological therapy cannot assure you that your symptoms will disappear. So none of these alternatives should ever be a substitute for drug therapy but should be used as an adjunct therapy to the main one.

Remember also that, some treatments, although natural, could still bring serious physical consequences if you do not know well the side effects nor the actual health status of those who will use them. So if you decide to use supplements or vitamins, remember that it is not enough that they are natural they must also be tested and then approved by the FDA (Food and Drug Administration).

Also, always remember to consult with your primary care physician before taking anything that has not been prescribed for you.

There is also to say that vitamin deficiency is caused precisely by the intake of some drugs used for ADHD therapy. For example, many stimulant drugs cause inappetence, which leads to eating much less and thus taking all the minerals and vitamins useful for the proper functioning of the body. These nutritional deficiencies, very often, are the cause of worsening clinical conditions of ADHD.

With that said, you will now be provided with a list of the best supplements and vitamins that are useful in combating ADHD symptoms.

- Zinc: Studies have found that children with ADHD have lower-than-normal levels of zinc within their bodies. Zinc is very useful in the regulation of dopamine, making methylphenidate more effective in the response that the nervous system gives after sending the same dopamine. Also according to these studies, it was shown that after taking zinc supplements, combined with traditional treatment for ADHD, these children had a marked improvement in symptoms. The improvement in symptoms was primarily related to that hyperactivity and impulsivity. However, during the research, no improvement was shown for one of the typical symptoms of ADHD: inattention.
- Omega-3 supplements: some research conducted by King's College of London and then published in the journal Neuropsychopharmacology have demonstrated the usefulness of omega-3 in combating the symptoms associated with ADHD. During the study conducted primarily on children between the ages of 8 and 12 who suffered from ADHD, it was highlighted that these subjects had low EPA, DHA and omega-3 levels. These studies have shown that omega-3s increase mental abilities in children between the ages of 8 and 12. Most importantly, a marked improvement in the organizational skills of children in this age group was found. In addition, thanks to omega-3s, cognitive function was improved, attention deficit disorder was reduced, and many behavioral disorders in ADHD sufferers were also corrected.
- Vitamin D: Much research in the United States has shown that children with ADHD have extremely low levels of vitamin D. It has also been shown that pregnant women who are vitamin D deficient are more likely to have a child with ADHD. Although there is no scientific evidence of improved conditions after vitamin D administration, it is a fact, however, that a deficiency of this important vitamin worsens the condition of those suffering from this disorder.

- Vitamin B: Vitamin B is essential for maintaining a healthy nervous system and digestive system, as well as being a valuable aid in various metabolic processes. It also plays a vital role in the executive functioning of the entire body. B vitamins are often used to reduce fatigue, improve moods, and improve attention deficit disorders. There are several subgroups of this vitamin that have in common, however, that they support and sustain the body and, in particular, the brain. Numerous studies, in which vitamin B was combined with the use of magnesium, have shown a decrease in anxiety and aggression, as well as a marked improvement in motility, in patients suffering from ADHD, and, in particular, in children affected by this disorder. One element belonging to the vitamin B subgroup, folate, is particularly essential in the improvement of ADHD symptoms. Folate is an essential element in the general detoxification process of the body in maintaining the integrity of DNA, keeping neurotransmissions active and being a support and regulator of the entire nervous system. Failure to regulate the nervous system coupled with malfunctioning neurotransmissions are the processes that underlie ADHD. Vitamin B supplementation is therefore vital, also because the human body can hardly synthesize these vitamins through food.
- Iron: Low iron levels are a fairly serious problem in ADHD patients. Various studies have shown the importance of iron for proper brain function. As a result, iron helps implement brain and cognitive functions that are often lacking in those who suffer from this disorder. Before you decide to take iron as a supplement to combat the symptoms of ADHD, however, it is necessary to check, through special blood tests, its value in the body. In particular, to understand if you have an iron deficiency, it is necessary to check the level of ferritin in the blood. Usually it is ferritin is at very low levels in those who suffer from ADHD. Usually to be at a borderline level and to supplement the level of ferritin must be lower than 30. As for the type of supplement it is essential that are used supplements based on chelated iron, to avoid gastro-intestinal problems. The recommended doses

are usually written in the package insert; however, the recommended dose is 30-40 mg per day for 3 months.
- Magnesium: This mineral has been shown to calm hyperactivity and agitation in ADHD sufferers. Magnesium is especially useful when the effect of stimulant medication begins to wear off. The recommended daily dose of magnesium ranges from 100 to 300 mg daily. The most commonly used forms of magnesium supplements are those in the form of magnesium citrate, chelate or glycinate.
- Ginko Biloba: Studies have shown that this herb, which has been used for hundreds of years to increase cognitive function, is very useful for improving ADHD symptoms. The Ginko Biloba plant contains substances known as terpene trillactones. These substances are very useful in protecting brain cells from damage and increasing the level of dopamine in the nervous system. During a scientific study, Ginko was added to the stimulant that is usually given to improve attention. Those who combined Ginko with the stimulant showed a 35% improvement in attention disorder. However, no improvement was shown in hyperactivity and impulsivity disorders. There is, in addition, another precaution to follow if you decide to use ginkgo Biloba as a supplement. This substance has strong anticoagulant effects, so it is strongly discouraged for those who suffer from circulation or blood clotting problems and, even more so, if they follow pharmacological therapy for blood clotting.
- Melatonin: Melatonin is a hormone responsible for regulating the sleep-wake cycle. This supplement is therefore very useful for all people who suffer from sleep disorders associated with ADHD. An adequate sleep associated with an adequate time of rest is very useful because it allows our organism to detoxify itself but also to allow a greater concentration during the day. Many scientific studies have shown that an adequate period of rest at night helps the brain to eliminate toxins accumulated during the day. Without an adequate period of rest, the toxins involved in neurodegenerative disorders accumulate in the free spaces of brain cells. Many times the cause of sleep disorders, or the worsening of these disorders, is associated with the

intake of stimulant medications used to treat ADHD. These stimulants act in a way that increases overall brain activity. Although stimulants are found to be very effective in improving the symptoms of ADHD very often these cause complaints such as difficulty falling asleep, difficulty waking up, waking up during the night hours with difficulty falling back asleep, sleepiness and fatigue throughout the day. In 2019, a study was conducted to evaluate the effects of melatonin in patients taking methylphenidate. The 74 study participants took melatonin for 4 weeks in a row. According to the reported results, about 61% of the participants showed marked improvements in sleep disturbances. In addition, many studies have shown how melatonin is supportive of the central nervous system in reducing inflammation of both chronic and acute origin.

- French maritime pine bark extract: This supplement contains natural extracts known as proanthocyanidins. The extract of this bark is usually found commercially under the registered trademark Pycnogenol. According to a study conducted in 2016, pine extract was found to be very helpful in alleviating some symptoms of ADHD. According to this study, pine bark extracts contain a high number of antioxidants, so this can reduce damage at the cellular level and also improves blood and oxygen flow to the brain. Increased oxygenation and cellular repair are behind the improvement of ADHD symptoms.

- Ginseng: Ginseng is a plant known to increase physical energy, stimulate brain function, and be very useful for improving intellectual and memory skills. Recently it has been discovered that this plant improves cognitive functions, such as attention, sensory functions, motor functions and reaction time. The effect of ginseng, in improving the symptoms of ADHD has been much studied, especially the beneficial effects on the disorder when this plant is used in combination with Ginko Biloba have been studied. It has also been discovered that, ginsenosides, constituent elements of the plant, increase concentration levels, at the level of the cerebral cortex, of both dopamine and noradrenaline. Thanks to these effects, it is thought that the long-term administration of ginseng may lead to neuro-cognitive

development in those people in whom the brain is not yet in a mature stage. They also help to improve attention disorders, hyperactivity and impulsivity.
- Rhodiola Rosea: it is a type of herb defined as adaptogenic, that is having neuroprotective properties and supports the correct functioning of the central nervous system. Adaptogens are also widely used for their ability to protect the body from various stress factors. Rhodiola Rosea increases brain function, stimulates the reticular activation system, improves the state of attention and vigilance, and increases the levels of dopamine, serotonin and norepinephrine which, as we know, are deficient in those suffering from ADHD. In addition, this type of medicinal herb has been found to improve many cognitive aspects, including attention, learning, stress, and fatigue.

Chapter 11: Sports Activity for Women with ADHD.

How exercise helps counteract ADHD symptoms

Practicing a sport, or physical activity consistently is very useful in promoting good health in many areas belonging to the central nervous system.

And while it's certainly good care for those who are in an excellent mental and physical state, it's even more so for those with ADHD.

Exercise is definitely one of the best non-clinical treatments that can be adopted by those with ADHD. And this is as true for children as it is for adults.

In fact, many scientific types of research that have focused on the association between exercise and ADHD have shown that practicing consistent physical activity, and consequently getting in good physical shape, helps improve cognitive abilities and ameliorate many of the symptoms of ADHD.

The benefits of engaging in physical activity when you have ADHD are far greater than for someone who does not have the disorder.

In fact, even a single workout session is enough to make you feel more motivated, increase your intellectual capacity, recharge and give you more energy, and make you feel less lost and confused.

Below you will find all the benefits you can have if you suffer from ADHD and decide to engage in any physical activity.

- Exercise increases the release of dopamine in the body. As we have already mentioned, dopamine is the neurotransmitter whose purpose is to promote feelings of pleasure and reward. Also, as we have reiterated many times, dopamine levels in ADHD sufferers are usually much lower than the normal threshold level. So one healthy way to increase dopamine levels in ADHD sufferers is to play sports on a regular basis. Being active at a physical level, therefore, is also very helpful in decreasing the drug therapy designed to stimulate dopamine

production. In any case, before making any changes to your therapeutic regimen, it is always best to consult your doctor.
- Exercise increases and improves executive function. Executive functions are a group of activities that are usually controlled by the frontal lobe. Among the various abilities are the ability to maintain focus and attention, the ability to manage time and people, the mnemonic ability and the ability to multitask. There are many ways to improve executive functions, and exercise is definitely one of the best ways to increase these abilities.
- Exercise succeeds in modifying brain-derived neurotrophic factor, or BDNF, signaling. BDNF is a brain molecule designed to increase learning and memory. According to some studies, BDNF malfunction is the main cause of the onset of ADHD. Therefore, a very effective way to increase BDNF production is to engage in physical activity. In fact, it was shown by a study conducted in 2016 that, the concentration of BDNF increased after practicing constant aerobic activity.
- Exercise helps regulate behavioral disorders and improve ADHD. Many people who suffer from ADHD show signs of hyperactivity. Exercise is therefore one of the best ways to vent and release all the physical energy that is being repressed. Therefore, thanks to exercise, antisocial behaviors such as anger, depression, impulsivity and aggression are corrected.

The best exercises for children and adolescents suffering from ADHD

During adolescence and preadolescence, purposeful exercise is less important than the actual time that is devoted to sports.

The Centers for Disease Control and Prevention, recommend that children and adolescents get at least 1 hour of physical activity daily to promote proper physical and mental development. And this talk is even more important for children and adolescents who suffer from ADHD.

The ideal physical activity for ADHD sufferers in this age group is:

- Take a bike ride for 60 minutes at a time, accompanied by family as well.
- Play a team sport such as basketball, soccer or baseball.
- Do fun aerobic sports such as jumping rope.
- Take hikes or long exploratory walks always accompanied by family.

The best exercises for adult women with ADHD

For adults, as well as children, physical activity is essential if you have ADHD.

As for adults, aerobic exercise is the best way to manage ADHD symptoms.

However, if you want to get more benefits from physical activity, especially if excess weight problems also arise, it would be much more useful to combine aerobic exercise with resistance exercise.

In addition, participating in diversified physical activities will allow you to increase your mental abilities as well, especially allowing you to improve the attention deficit typical of those suffering from ADHD. When it comes to choosing an exercise that is truly effective you will need to ensure that it has a moderately high level of intensity. This means that your ideal workout should increase your heart rate, increase the intensity of your breathing, make you sweat, and make your muscles feel tired. A very helpful tip to see if your workout falls within these parameters is to use a heart rate monitor.

The best exercises to do in your specific case are:
- Cycling.
- Crossfit.
- HIIT.
- Spinning.
- Boxing.
- Cycling.
- Jogging.

Either way, it doesn't matter what type of exercise you decide to pursue. The important thing is to move, do something you love, release tension and recharge your mind.

One very important piece of advice that you should definitely follow is to vary your exercise routine. This way you will avoid both getting bored and easily distracted from your task, thus losing interest very easily and leaving your exercise plan halfway through. You can also change exercises even during your dedicated hour of training, doing a certain type of exercise in the first thirty minutes and totally changing exercises in the other 30 minutes.

Another very useful tip, to keep you motivated and compelled to do the exercises, is to follow the exercise program with another person, whether it is your partner, friend or family member. This will not only keep you motivated, but in case you get discouraged and decide to quit, it will help you to stay attentive and present to the commitment you made.

Sport concludes our comprehensive practical guide to better lifestyle management for adult woman with ADHD. The fifth part of the text, however, will see the management of the disease from a purely mental point of view: in fact, we will talk about effective daily routines, Mindfulness and meditations useful for ADHD and other relaxation techniques such as those typical of Yoga to help you manage even the most negative emotions.

Part Five: Managing ADHD from a purely mental perspective

Chapter 12: The Importance of Meditation

As we have seen several times in this guide, ADHD is a disorder that compromises the main life contexts of the person with this disorder, as, for example, it happens in the school context during the developmental stage and then moves on to the family and the social and work context during adulthood.

According to the American Psychiatric Association, for a person to be considered to have ADHD, he or she must have developed symptoms within the first 12 years of life, have these symptoms active consecutively for 6 months, and these symptoms must have negative impacts on at least two aspects of the affected person's life.

ADHD is also broken down into three main categories:
- Inattentive, which affects between 20 and 30 percent of sufferers.
- Hyperactive-impulsive which affects about 15% of those with ADHD.
- A combined subtype, which affects between 50 and 75 percent of ADHD sufferers.

The degeneration of the disorder occurs when the symptoms are not treated adequately and are not dealt with following a multimodal scheme, that is, according to a scheme that integrates psychotherapy, pharmacological therapy and the use of educational strategies based both on the person and on the context of life in which the person suffering from ADHD is integrated.

To date, therefore, ADHD sufferers are treated with different therapies or multidisciplinary therapies. However, it has recently been shown that complementary alternative medicine therapies play a fairly decisive role in the clinical treatment of this disorder. In fact, integrated mind-body therapies, are the ones that are currently most used for the treatment of ADHD, especially approaches based on Mindfulness and meditation are used. These approaches cause significant improvement in psychological, social, emotional and neurobiological functioning in those who suffer from this disorder.

These new techniques use meditation or deep breathing to enhance the field of self-awareness using tools such as relaxation, guided imagery techniques, and yoga.

It has been demonstrated that practicing this kind of therapy can help a lot in modifying some patterns of activation of the brain, also help to reduce anxiety, stress and pain sensation as well as to develop concentration and attention and greater control of inhibitory skills. This happens thanks to particular neurophysiological mechanisms that activate the dopaminergic and noradrenergic systems.

Multidimensional behavioral therapies-those therapies that bring together exercise and aerobic activity, deep breathing, meditation, and mental and physical balancing-help to sharply regulate the emotional responses of those with ADHD.

Application of Mindfulness in ADHD

Mindfulness is defined as the ability to place attention intentionally, in the present moment, and a non-judgmental manner. These three components allow the person undergoing therapy to relate in a mindful way to their experiences, with the attitude of always being present to themselves but in an uncritical, non-anxious way.

Mindfulness stands as a technique that strengthens the mind's ability to control itself and its capacity for attention. It also teaches how to observe one's own behavior and how to focus on something in particular or on a specific task. And it teaches how to go back and bring the mind back to the exact moment it is distracted from the concentration task assigned to it.

Mindfulness stands as a basic principle to control ADHD in children, adolescents and adults and all three subtypes of the disorder. Mindfulness thus constitutes physical training designed to reactivate the mechanisms of attention.

The positive effects of this type of therapy are found particularly on inattention, hyperactivity, impulsivity and all those skills that are related to speed, accuracy and reaction time.

Secondary results were found to improve anxiety disorders, disorders related to excessive shyness and subsequent self-closure, problems related to socialization, excessive perfectionism, emotional dysregulation, and depressive symptoms.

Mindfulness, therefore, helps to greatly develop skills such as acceptance, awareness, and focus.

Moreover, based above all on the attitude of non-judgment, even aspects that belong strictly to the behavioral sphere can have positive implications, ensuring that those suffering from ADHD develop positive feelings such as patience, tolerating waiting or bearing even the most frustrating moments with optimism.

In the application of Mindfulness techniques, it is imperative that in addition to the young person suffering from ADHD, the adults who surround the sufferer of this disorder are also involved in the therapy. Training parents improve their understanding of this disorder and the behavioral problems that are related to this disorder, helping them to find and implement more effective strategies.

The psycho-educational phases of the disorder and the techniques used in the Mindfulness protocol have positive effects both in practical terms and in terms of the general well-being of family relationships, reinforcing, at the same time, compliance with the treatment and continuing to practice the exercises at home once the treatment is over.

Attention regulation and reeducation through Mindfulness follow four basic aspects:

- Sustained attention regulation aimed at maintaining awareness of the experience obtained in the present moment.

- Attention redirection, allows sufferers to bring attention back after a distraction.
- Inhibition of the elaborative process, which allows you to avoid ruminating on thoughts or feelings that are not relevant to the present moment.
- Undirected attention, is useful for improving awareness of present experiences, experiences that should not be influenced by either assumptions or expectations.

The Transcendental Meditation method to combat ADHD

Recently a new non-pharmacological method has been introduced in the treatment of ADHD, tested and implemented thanks to the studies carried out by Dr. Sarina Grosswald: the use of the technique of Transcendental Meditation Maharishi.

The Transcendental Meditation technique can prove to be a valuable and powerful aid in the treatment of both children and adults suffering from ADHD.

This type of meditation technique, unlike the use of drugs, does not treat the symptoms of the disorder but helps to influence in a positive way the underlying causes of the disease. This means that, unlike drug therapy, it does not create an improvement in purely temporary disorders but improves the symptoms permanently.

What does this type of meditation technique consist of in practice? The Transcendental Meditation technique is a unique meditation methodology. Basically, it's a very simple meditation process that allows the mind to calm down and allows for a state of restful alertness. When the mind enters this state the body also relaxes in a profound way. Gradually the thought enters a state of stillness, the mind then transcends from active mental activity and a state of deep silence is experienced.

Thanks to this activity, a state of mental calm are achieved that ADHD sufferers rarely experience. In studies conducted by Dr. Grosswald, she was able to observe a significant reduction in stress in people suffering from ADHD.

This state of deep calm also leads to positive changes in both the physiological and neuropsychological realms. These changes lead to integration and coherence in the functioning of the entire nervous system. Moreover, thanks to this technique, more and more connections are created in the areas located at the frontal level of the nervous system, which are the areas that control impulsiveness, discernment and interpersonal relationships.

So the Transcendental Meditation technique by reducing stress and optimizing brain functioning is very helpful in reducing the typical symptoms of ADHD.

On the practical side, it should be noted that this technique is so simple that both adults and children suffering from ADHD can practice it easily and without any particular effort. In fact, this type of meditation does not require any particular concentration or mind control, nor any particular changes in one's lifestyle or in the lifestyle of children suffering from ADHD. The technique consists of practicing meditation twice a day for a period of time ranging from 10 to 20 minutes. As for the position, it will be enough to simply sit with your eyes closed.

According to a study published in Mind and Brain, the Journal of Psychiatry, published in July 2011, children who practiced Transcendental Meditation showed more than a 50% reduction in ADHD symptoms, as well as reductions in symptoms such as stress, anxiety and depression. In addition, these children showed increased concentration and focus, improved temperament, and better control of impulsivity. Another positive finding of this study was provided by the teachers who had these ADHD children in their classrooms. The teachers stated that after beginning meditation sessions, they were able to teach with much greater ease and profit. Pupils with ADHD, on the other hand, being less stressed and less anxious, were more attentive and more independent and were able to perform their duties, such as homework, with greater ease.

To conclude the speech, we can say that Transcendental Meditation, even if it is not completely resolving the problem, can make a great contribution to improving the quality of life of those suffering from ADHD.

How yoga can help combat ADHD

Scientific research, based primarily on studies conducted over the past 10 years, has shown that yoga can be an important tool to better manage ADHD.

In fact, research has shown that yoga is one of the few non-medical treatments that are very effective in controlling the symptoms of ADHD because this discipline promotes the development and connection between mind and body.

A study conducted by the Mayo Clinic recognized that the practice of yoga is a very useful way to alleviate, especially in combination with psychotherapy and drug therapy, diet and lifestyle modification, the symptoms of ADHD.

Therefore, it is very likely that education policy may find it useful to associate yoga as a therapy in both school and family settings, as well as a management tool for the adult person who is to enter the workforce.

As we said, the main purpose of yoga is to create harmony between the physical, psychic and affective dimensions of the human being. A person who practices yoga, even beginners, will soon begin to follow a technique that will lead him to have a greater state of attention and concentration, with subsequent development in inhibitory management, thus leading him to better manage both their emotional components and the contexts in which he will have to interact. Children and adults who suffer from this disorder are very often unable to connect body and mind, and it is yoga that can help in a clear way to create this connection.

In terms of managing ADHD, the most useful techniques are asanas (or postures), pranayama (or breathing techniques), and dhyana (or meditation techniques).

Some asanas are in fact able to provide a greater flow of blood and oxygen to the brain, which has a balancing effect on the internal nervous system.

A recent study, led by Professor Sergey Kiselev, head of the Department of Neurocognitive and Brain Development at Ural University, showed that yoga, especially meditation and breathing techniques, helped develop concentration in children with ADHD.

During the study, the 16 participating children, ages 6 to 7, practiced breathing and meditative exercises for 3 months, 3 times a week. The researchers' goal was to see what effect body-oriented training might have on the mental functions needed to complete a task in children with ADHD. Specifically, they wanted to verify that, yoga exercises based on meditation and breathing, could develop the ability to concentrate in children with ADHD.

Results from this study showed that yoga developed and improved executive skills (those, in essence, involved in completing a task) in children with ADHD. The positive effects were seen both immediately at the end of the study and in the months that followed. Also according to this study, through breathing exercises, cerebral oxygenation was improved, leading to better reticular function, while through the regular practice of asanas, regulation and control functions were improved.

Other recent studies, in addition to confirming Dr. Kiselev's study, have shown that the consistent practice of yoga helps develop and strengthen memory levels, another of the very common symptoms of ADHD sufferers.

Yoga also helps to control and reduce the impulsivity typical of ADHD sufferers. Usually, and especially in the pre-adolescent phase, those who suffer from ADHD are very impatient and usually lose calm or attention very easily. The maintenance of some asanas, associated with breathing techniques, is very useful to develop self-control and especially to control negative emotions such as anxiety, stress, impulsiveness and anger. In addition, the constant control of impulsivity will greatly improve social relations and relationships with the surrounding environment in those suffering from ADHD.

Yoga will also help improve the self-esteem of those who suffer from this disorder. It is known that those who suffer from ADHD have a fairly significant deterioration in their quality of life. The deterioration leads, as a logical consequence, to strong self-esteem problems. Thanks to yoga, slowly you will have full control of your emotions, thus increasing the esteem and confidence in yourself and your abilities.

Regarding the constant practice of this activity, it is recommended, especially for those who suffer from this disorder, to find an experienced and very prepared instructor. It is, therefore, necessary not only to have a lot of experience in the practice of yoga, but it is especially necessary to look for an instructor who has experience both with children, and especially who has experience with adults and children who suffer from attention disorder or hyperactivity.

What are the benefits of meditative methods in those with ADHD

The theoretical data that have reached us from the various studies carried out on meditation and ADHD is certainly positive. In fact, it has been shown that meditation helps those suffering from ADHD mainly because it gives a strong contribution to the thickening of the prefrontal cortex. This area of the nervous system is involved in the processes of focusing, planning events, and controlling impulsivity. Another effect of meditation is increasing dopamine levels in the brain, a neurotransmitter that is almost absent in the brains of those with ADHD.

A study conducted by the University of UCLA showed that people suffering from ADHD, who participated in meditation sessions at least once a week and for about 2 hours and 30 minutes and then continued to meditate at home, gradually increasing the time of concentration from 5 to 15 minutes, after 8 weeks of practice, showed both effective improvements in concentration and the ability to complete daily tasks that were assigned to them. In addition, the people involved in the study showed a dramatic reduction in depressive symptoms and anxiety disorders.

In addition to these benefits, this technique can help increase self-esteem, reduce stress, and even help with weight loss in those who also suffer from ADHD-related weight issues. As far as weight is concerned, in fact, those who suffer from ADHD very often also pay little attention to what they eat, as they are unable to focus on eating. Meditation helps you in this regard, as it encourages you to pay much more attention to everything you do, including eating healthily and properly.

Here we conclude the management of ADHD from a mental perspective through meditation, yoga, and mindfulness techniques. The next part of the text will be just as important because it will cover managing emotional relationships for women with ADHD. From the sexual sphere to family or friendly relationships, you will be shown how to manage your social life and especially make you realize that despite having such a socially compromising condition, it is possible for you to have a healthy and full relational life.

Part Six: How to manage relationships if you have ADHD

Chapter 13: Relationship Management for the Woman with ADHD.

Relational problems associated with ADHD

As we all know, ADHD can cause problems from small to very difficult to manage in the emotional sphere and consequently in the affective sphere. In fact, frustration, resentment and lack of empathy towards others can arise, almost always leading to unjustified arguments and many times to the interruption of emotional relationships.

Symptoms such as hyperactivity, disorganization, and impulsivity create the woman suffering from ADHD various problems in various spheres of adult life. However, these symptoms can be even more damaging and detrimental when it comes to romantic relationships. And it is especially damaging if these symptoms have never been diagnosed and treated clinically.

If you suffer from ADHD, you often suffer from negative feelings and sensations, such as feeling frequently criticized, constantly nagged, and filled with guilt over situations that are very often out of your control. No matter what you do, nothing seems to please your partners or your friends and family. Very often you feel mistreated by those around you and controlled in every aspect of your life.

Conversely, the person in the life of an individual with ADHD often feels alone, ignored and unappreciated. In addition, those who do not suffer from this disorder, are very unlikely to be willing to tolerate for long those who do not keep their promises and never carry out any of the demands made on them.

Even with regard to the sphere of relationships concerning friendship, for those suffering from ADHD, it is really difficult to find friends or to manage, in any case, to maintain long-term friendships. It's easy to see how conflicting feelings and needs often lead to broken relationships.

But you don't necessarily always have to come to the end of relationships. If you suffer from ADHD, you may very well be able to establish healthy social and romantic relationships by implementing simple strategies that will improve the situation.

Helpful tips on how to improve your romantic relationship with your partner if you have ADHD

The first step you need to take, in order to make a positive change in your relationship, is to understand what role your disorder plays within your relationship.

Once you understand and identify which symptoms are interfering the most in your relationship, you can adopt the best strategies to be able to manage them. Basically, you should learn what are the best strategies to manage your symptoms.

The following will provide you with some strategies to better manage some of the major symptoms that cause problems within your couple's life.

Distraction and difficulty paying attention

Distraction is the primary and characteristic symptom of those ADHD. Women suffering from ADHD seem to have great difficulty in listening to their partners and as a result, fail to understand their needs. Although you actually love your partner immensely, your attention deficit will often lead you to ignore them. Your partner will then feel alone and misunderstood.

Very often, then, during conversations, your tendency to get distracted will lead you to miss chunks of conversations with important details, forgetting even the requests that have been made of you.

One tip to be able to remedy this problem is to be clear, right from the start. Talk openly with your partner about your disorder and if conversations start to get long and you start to get distracted politely ask your partner to take breaks or repeat if you got distracted and didn't understand or listen to what was said.

Hyperfocus

Another one of the typical symptoms of ADHD is hyperfocus, which is paying uninterrupted, exaggerated attention to an activity you are doing. Very often, you become so absorbed in these activities that you find it difficult and sometimes painful to take your attention away from what you are doing. If hyperfocus is an advantage at the productivity level, it is definitely not in your couple's life, as it may make your partner feel unwanted and less important than whatever gets your attention.

The advice to remedy this problem is actually quite simple: avoid focusing on any activity that can completely absorb your thoughts when it's time for you to interact with your partner.

A very useful way to selectively allocate time to your activities and your partner is to set a timer, even with your cell phone, that tells you the exact time you need to complete your task.

Or, when you realize that you are entering a state of total absence from reality, focusing your attention only on a certain activity, get up and start walking, so as to break this vicious circle.

Disorganization

When you have ADHD, it can often happen that you forget to do a task in the home environment, such as forgetting to do household chores or starting a job and never completing it.

Or you may have lost the keys to your house or car, lost important documents, or kept some object and can no longer find it because you do not remember where you put it.

Disorganization is definitely one of the most negative aspects in the lives of ADHD sufferers because it causes not only an excessive amount of time wasted but many times a huge amount of money lost as well.

Solving this problem certainly requires the help of a specialist, but there are small steps in the life of a couple that can be implemented to mitigate the situation.

For example, you can take on chores within your home life that don't require organizational burdens, such as doing laundry or taking care of the kitchen, rather than paying taxes or bills.

Also, when you decide to put something in order, given your tendency also to forget the exact location of items, you could keep a journal where you make a list of the items and the place where you have placed them.

Impulsivity

Usually, women who suffer from hyperactivity, simultaneously also develop the subtype of impulsivity. So it will often occur to you to act without first thinking.

Among the common problems that plague the life of a couple is impulsive and compulsive shopping. You often spend money on things you don't need and just as often manage to spend more than you can afford.

Impulsivity also leads you to other types of extreme situations, such as having promiscuous sex without any kind of precautions, or driving dangerously, often becoming a risk to yourself but also to others.

Self-control is a mental discipline that can be learned easily. Disciplines that help you take control of your body and mind, such as yoga and meditation in general, can be very helpful to you in managing your deleterious behaviors. They can also help you manage your behaviors in the social sphere so that you do not fall back into the middle of rather unpleasant situations. Or, they can be very helpful in dealing with the impulsiveness of constantly interrupting your partner during a conversation.

However, if your impulsive attitudes are completely out of control, the only solution is to see a psychotherapist.

Procrastination

Endlessly putting off a task or never completing a task is another key element that leads to the breakdown of romantic relationships. People who suffer from ADHD, not only have the problem of procrastinating on tasks that need to be done, but very often they also have difficulty starting a project or feel overwhelmed by the project itself. Or you find that you need to get to the end of the project to feel motivated to start and complete it. All of these attitudes, very often are poorly tolerated by your partner, resulting in a painful decision by your partner to terminate your relationship.

If your problem is putting off a project indefinitely, the solution might be to divide said project into many small projects. Start with the first part of the project and avoid focusing on the rest of the project. And if you still feel overwhelmed, quietly ask your partner to help you in completing it.

Mood swings

People who suffer from ADHD often have serious difficulties managing their emotions. More often than not, you will have experienced bouts of anger or frequent, uncontrolled mood swings throughout the day. This is because your disorder causes you to amplify normal emotions that can be interjected into your daily routine.

And while the situation is depressing enough for you, for your partner it becomes something unmanageable.

Mood swings very often are also caused by the bad habits you tend to adopt.

To improve this condition following a healthy and proper lifestyle, ranging from diet to exercise, can be of great help to you.

Disciplines such as yoga or taichi can help you with stress and anger management.

Also, a good way to make your partner understand your condition and strengthen your relationship would be to engage in physical activities, such as hiking and walking outdoors, together.

How to improve the sexual sphere if you suffer from ADHD

The sexual sphere, such as having sexual and satisfying relationships with one's partner, is a very common problem in women suffering from ADHD. Some of these symptoms affect the sexual sphere leading to dysfunction as well. All this can cause strong states of stress within a couple, very often leading to the very termination of the relationship.

As we have said many times, people who suffer from ADHD have a much more developed level of sensitivity than the norm. If we include this aspect in the sexual life of a woman who suffers from ADHD we have as a result that sexual activities, which create pleasant situations for those who do not suffer from this disorder, can be experienced as unpleasant and sometimes even stressful and traumatizing.

Those with ADHD often find situations that can cause pleasure, such as smells, tactile sensations, and being touched as disgusting and unpleasant.

In addition, because of being super critical of oneself and the low self-esteem that ADHD sufferers experience, it is often difficult to have sex with one's partner.

Identifying the specific symptom that is causing you to have these difficulties in your life is quite complicated because those with ADHD many times exhibit specific symptoms that are not common in other individuals.

However, there are specific categories under which difficulties in sexuality fall, which are:

- Hyposexuality: many women who suffer from ADHD very often show a tendency to have no interest in sex. They may also have difficulty concentrating during the sexual act, lose interest in the middle of the sexual activity itself, or become very easily distracted by what they are doing. Many times, the problem of ADHD hyposexuality is exacerbated by drug therapy prescribed by your primary care physician.
- Hypersexuality: in contrast to hyposexuality, hypersexuality leads to an extremely high sex drive. Sexual intercourse allows

for the release of endorphins, giving that state of calm that ADHD sufferers sorely need. For this reason, many women who suffer from ADHD can run into risky sexual practices, precisely because of excessive impulsivity.
- Inability to reach orgasm: while some women who suffer from ADHD show no interest in sexual activity, others are very attracted to it. However, for many women suffering from this disorder, it is almost impossible to achieve orgasm. This problem is often linked to the lack of concentration and hyperactivity typical of ADHD. Again, in addition to the typical symptoms, the lack of pleasure may be related to the medications you are taking.
- Hypersensitivity: many women with ADHD develop a kind of physical hypersensitivity that causes them to resent anything associated with physical contact. And this translates to hypersensitivity even in the genital area, often making sexual intercourse unpleasant or even painful. This leads, as a consequence to an immediate loss of interest in the sexual act.
- Hyperactivity: hyperactivity also affects the sexual sphere of a woman suffering from ADHD. This is because, those who suffer from hyperactivity have a lot of difficulties relaxing and stretching. They may also feel the need to have to constantly change positions or be unable to concentrate for long periods, causing them to lose interest in what they are doing.

How to overcome difficulties in the sexual arena if you have ADHD

There are many techniques you can learn and use, such as coping techniques, that will help you remove the specific difficulties you have in the sexual arena if you have ADHD.

Here are some practical tips you can easily put into practice to improve your sex life.

Learn to communicate

Communication is vital in a couple's life, particularly in the couple's life of those with ADHD.

Talking about your sexual issues with your partner will help you both understand each other better and manage your relationships better. And it's also a very helpful way to ease the tension if you're early in the relationship. Although communicating with those with ADHD many times seems to be overly difficult, expressing openly and honestly what your needs and struggles are can be helpful to you as it may create more intimacy and prompt your partner to go the extra mile to put you at ease.

Remove all distractions

While for normal people a little music to set the mood, dim lights, or candles can be seen as relaxing and exciting, for those with ADHD they can be distracting. Turning off anything that might get your attention and distract you from sex is definitely the best solution.

However, ADHD sufferers are not only distracted by material things that are present in the room at the time. More often than not, the distraction is only in the mental sphere, as while you are in the intimate moment, you get caught up in distant thoughts, such as work, home, or children. All thoughts definitely do not help you focus on intimacy. Again, communication is a good starting point to solve your problem. Speak to your partner clearly by saying what is distracting you, both materially and mentally, so as to remove all possible sources of distraction.

You often make changes in the sexual sphere as well

With this, we do not want to advise you to change partners often, but rather to make changes regarding for example positions, or places where you are used to practicing relationships. All this will help you with your tendency to easily lose interest in anything that turns out to be monotonous and lacking in stimulation.

Try to communicate your needs, reminding your partner that for you, constantly changing routines can help you both have a healthy and fulfilling sex life.

Focus on being present

Attention deficit disorder is definitely one of the most annoying symptoms, both for you and those around you, of ADHD. Strive to stay focused in all ways on what you are doing and what is happening at that very moment. All of this will help your mind to digress and lose focus and therefore excitement.

To learn how to focus and be less distracted you could take meditation classes and attend yoga classes, where you will learn how to focus, manage stress, and stay mindful of what you are doing.

If you practice yoga and meditation before sexual intercourse with your partner, it can help calm your mind, allowing you to practice being intimate with your partner in a more relaxed way.

Learn to program

Many times, the easiest solution to not having intimate problems with your partner is to set a schedule and try to stick to it as faithfully as possible.

Although for many people who don't suffer from your disorder scheduling may seem like something unromantic and sometimes mechanical, in your case writing and setting a goal is definitely vital. This is because, it will help you focus your attention on one thought and one goal and it will also help you relieve the stress and anxiety that haunts you, especially when you think you are clumsy or inadequate.

How to raise and manage your children if you have ADHD

Being a mom is one of the hardest jobs for a woman. The job is much harder if, in addition to being a mom, you also suffer from

ADHD. Not to consider how debilitating your condition can be if, in addition to being a mom, you also have a full-time job.

On top of that, your disorder never leads you to be satisfied with your work, even as a mom. Which leads you to always be critical of yourself, or to always feel effectively criticized by those around you because you fail to pay proper attention to your children. All this will make you feel perpetually frustrated and dissatisfied, making you always believe that you are a bad example and especially a bad parent.

Having ADHD does not automatically make you a bad mother. On the contrary, more often than not your disorder may cause you to enter into a greater state of empathy with your children while creating a loving and welcoming family environment. In fact, remember that, for a child, it matters little whether your home is polished to perfection. All a child cares about is being loved.

There are some very useful tips, which you will find below, that will help you to cope more serenely and live with your disorder, and at the same time make you feel like a good parent.

Accept your disorder

The first piece of advice is to quietly accept that you have ADHD. Once you become aware of your problem, you will realize that the image of a woman who has to take care of the needs of others at the expense of her own, or who has to be perfect in all situations is absolutely wrong.

Start asking for help

Once you have accepted your disorder and, more importantly, once you understand that no one is perfect and infallible, start asking your family members for help. In addition to taking some huge burdens off of you, asking for help will also teach you to understand what a sense of responsibility actually is. Also, remember that a family only functions well and solves problems and conflicts when you all work together. Another tip is not to feel guilty if you accept outside help, such as someone to help with cleaning or a babysitter if you work full time. This will give you more time for yourself while easing all the tensions that arise in the family when you are under stress.

Find a space of your own and relax
Your disorder very often leads you to be stressed and disorganized even when it comes to managing your home and children.

A good tip is to start your day by carving out a small space of time all to yourself. During this time, you could try meditation and relaxation techniques and then carve out some of this time to make a list and plan out in detail all the tasks you need to do throughout the day.

Do the same thing the night before you go to sleep, relax for 15 minutes, and if you don't think you have time in the morning to plan events, do it the night before.

Plan meals and events in advance
Very often it happens that, because of anxiety and disorganization, especially when dealing with young children, you tend to forget meals and bedtimes, risking overfeeding your children in an unhealthy way. Or many times you forget to change a diaper or let your child take a nap.

So plan meal times and nap or bath times, and also, if you have a tendency to forget a diaper change, make a note to do it at least once before naptime.

Hire a teacher
If you often find that you can't keep up with your children's homework, you may want to consider hiring a teacher. This will help your children learn better and be less stressed by the more difficult tasks. It will also lighten a fairly heavy workload for you, making sure that you are free to devote yourself to cooking or the rest of the chores, without making you feel guilty for neglecting your children's schooling.

Learn not to make unrealistic promises
You are often tempted, because of frustration at feeling like a bad parent all the time, to make promises that you know are impossible to keep, to compensate for what you believe are parental shortcomings.

Or children make crazy demands on you and you promise to accommodate all their whims to make yourself feel better.

So try not to promise anything that is out of your reach, and above all try to understand and make your children understand that affection is more important than material goods.

Doing something important and nice for your children will definitely be much better than promising something and then not delivering it.

With this speech ends the sixth part of the book. The seventh part of the manual, however, will be an economic part, which is purely about work and how to manage work relationships and your work with this disease but also a guide on how to manage money. You will therefore find tips on money and savings.

Part Seven: How to manage work and money for the woman with ADHD

Chapter 14: Work issues for the woman with ADHD.

Women, work and ADHD: some statistics

You will often have read during your job search that employers looking for employees are usually looking for people with organizational speed, care, and attention to detail, or focus on excellent business goals. But for you who suffer from ADHD, it's really tricky to fit into these expectations. And not only does it make the task of finding a job very difficult for you, but very often, once you get it you will find it difficult to excel or maintain expectations to the point where you lose your job for good.

It is estimated that between 8 and 9 million American adults suffer from ADHD. Among those millions is a huge chunk that belongs to the female gender. A nationwide survey determined that only 50% of adults with ADHD are able to hold down a steady, stable job, compared to 72% of the normal adult population.

Moreover, once they got the job, it was difficult for many of them to get promotions or the same salary level as their peers. And the female situation was definitely worse than the male one.

The level of influence ADHD has in the workplace depends a lot on how severe your disorder is, and more importantly, whether or not you are addressing the situation pharmacologically and therapeutically.

For some people with ADHD, it may be simply difficult to sit still and concentrate in the workplace, or for others, it is difficult to get through the day, while for others with severe anger management issues, it is difficult to maintain good relationships with colleagues to the point of actual physical or verbal confrontations.

All of this often leads to job loss, continual change of employment, and loss of any kind of government benefits once left without employment.

The most common problems that arise in the work environment when you have ADHD are:

- Poor management of work hours.
- Being able to organize your work.
- Being able to finish work or meet goals.
- Difficulty listening to directions and paying attention during work meetings.
- Follow the directions for performing your duties.
- Difficulty paying attention to the details of the work to be done.
- Often arriving late to work, or leaving before others.
- Failing to not interrupt during a meeting or a supervisor explaining how to do your job.
- Sitting for long periods of time.
- Being able to curb anger, stress, rage, and anxiety.

In the work environment, ADHD very often leads to anxiety disorders and depressive syndromes, as well as accentuating low self-esteem, significantly worsening your already troubled psycho-physical situation.

Practical tips on how to get and keep a job

If you suffer from low self-esteem, problems with concentration, or managing impulsivity, the first step is always to consult a specialist doctor or a psychotherapist, who will provide you with all the tools best suited to manage your disorder.

But there are some useful little tricks that will help you in carrying out your work activities, without wasting useful time so that you not only lose your job but also easily find one that meets your needs.

- See an employment consultant. If you are looking for a job and do not know where to start, good advice is to consult an employment consultant, who will certify what are your skills and what are your limits and will be able to suggest which job is best suited to your needs and specific characteristics. He or she may also be able to help you in your search for a job that has more flexible hours or with situations that do not involve exacerbating states of anxiety or excessively heavy or stressful work.

- Personalize your workspace. Another useful tip to succeed once you get the job and avoid losing it abruptly is to personalize your work environment. This way, you will be able to focus on the strengths that set you apart at work and minimize the negatives as much as possible. It would also be very useful to find a quiet space so that you can work with serenity without being constantly distracted by your surroundings.
- Find someone to help you and learn to delegate. It would be very helpful to find an assistant so that you can delegate to them the tasks that are more difficult or less necessary for you to perform your duties properly.
- Keep a note of all your commitments. Even at work, taking notes and keeping track of things to do can be extremely helpful. So keep a diary, even a digital one, where you will mark a list of things to do at work on a daily basis. Also, you can configure your smartphone or computer to send you some sort of alarm as a reminder of the tasks you have to do.
- Take notes. Again because of the attention deficit, one tip for not getting distracted during business meetings and forgetting what to do is to take as many notes as possible.
- Plan your workday in advance. Another way to perform your tasks to the best of your ability and not get distracted during the workday is to section off the tasks you need to do throughout the day. Then set aside a specific time, perhaps right at the beginning of the workday, to answer calls and emails so you don't have to constantly interrupt the work you are doing.
- Try to set easy and realistic goals. Don't try to overdo it at work, starting lots of projects and not completing any of them. As we have told you, a good way to accomplish all the tasks you have been assigned is to divide your workday into several parts. In this way, once you have started one project and planned the

next, it will be impossible for you to be distracted by other projects and not finish the one you just started. To understand when it is time to stop one task and start another other it would be very useful to set a timer or use the timer on your smartphone.
- Learn how to relax and manage stress. Relaxation techniques, as we have seen throughout the discussion of this guide, are a real boon for those with ADHD. Learning how to relax and manage stress will be very helpful during the long work days you face. Take time to practice deep breathing and meditation before you go to work and once you get home to relieve tension. Or, during working hours, try to find ways to relax during your breaks, such as talking with colleagues about topics other than work, or reading a magazine or a book.

Chapter 15: Money Management for the Woman with ADHD

Tips on how to manage money

Many women who suffer from ADHD have great difficulty managing money, as the financial side requires a lot of attention to detail, time and focus that definitely don't go along with your disorder.
Very often you will have spent too much money, many times even beyond your financial means, and therefore find yourself very often short of money.
The following will provide you with helpful tips on how to manage money without finding yourself full of debt.
With these tips, it will be much easier for you to manage your financial assets without spending more than you have to being denied a loan or financing because you forgot to pay some installments, or often having a bank account in the red.

Try to understand where your money is going

If you suffer from compulsive shopping, keeping a list of what you need to buy will ensure that you don't overbuy, buying things that are completely unnecessary.
Keeping a planner of all expenses and purchases made will give you a better understanding of where most of your money is going.
Always carry a small notebook or use an app with an expense planner and jot down all of your purchases, even the ones that seem small and insignificant to you.
Although it is stressful for you to have to mark down everything you spend, it is helpful for your trouble. In fact, the information you gather will help you improve your money management habits.
Also, it would be very helpful if you mark all the fixed expenses like bills or taxes and subscriptions in your planner. This way, you can do a calculation of the fixed expenses with the occasional ones and, if you realize that you are exceeding your available monthly budget, you can figure out what is unnecessary and cut those extra expenses.

Try to identify what your goals are, both short-term and long-term

Make a list of all your priorities, whether they are making major purchases for your new home, or paying off debt. With that done, figure out what to start cutting back on and how to find an alternative, such as avoiding eating out a lot or bringing your own food from home when you go to work, so you can save money and set aside the money you need for your bigger purposes.

Try to organize your financial practices

The key to being able to best manage your attention deficit is to simplify things as much as possible. This also applies in the financial area. If you also have organizational problems, the solution is to keep folders and file cabinets, labeled by month and day, in which you must enter deadlines and payments made. As soon as you receive a tax or utility bill, open it immediately and enter the day and month in which you need to pay it. The advice, however, is to enter it at least 4-5 days before the actual due date, so that you don't always fall back to the last moment.

Save your expense receipts

Learn to set aside all receipts for expenses and payments, and not to throw away receipts either. Provide yourself with a magazine rack or a set of folders where you should put all the receipts and bills you accumulate during the day. Then divide the receipts between those you need to figure out how much money you spent on your purchases from those you need for tax deductions.

As you throw away anything superfluous and unnecessary.

At the end of the month, take all the receipts you have accumulated and put them in a folder with the month and year written on it. Put the folder in an archive and this way you will have an up-to-date and perfectly cataloged database. This way, if you need a receipt, proof of purchase, a warranty for a product, or the balance of payment, you'll have it all under control and readily at your fingertips.

Get advice from a financial expert

However, if you are unable to manage your accounts and finances on your own, don't be afraid to consult an expert in the field. In fact, an expert's advice could help you understand what expenses to avoid, or how best to invest your money to avoid excessive losses that could even lead to bankruptcy.

If your job and finances can afford it, the advice is to engage the services of an experienced accountant or financial adviser. They can help you manage and plan for any financial issues that you may not be able to handle on your own.

Try to save some money for when you retire

If you are working and suffer from ADHD, you will often run out of all the money available to you by the end of the financial year. This way, aside from what your company sets aside for retirement, you will effectively find yourself with very little money left over when you finish working.

Learning to put something aside and not spend your entire paycheck could be very helpful once you stop working.

The ideal solution, if you are not good at managing your money, would be to transfer even a small part of it to an account that is separate from yours and locked, so that you are not tempted to withdraw that amount as well and spend it.

Money management tips conclude the penultimate part of this handbook. In the next and final part of the text we will provide you with more practical tips and guidance on how to manage time for an adult woman with ADHD.

Part Eight - Time Management Tips

Chapter 16: Some useful and practical techniques for having a good general demeanor with ADHD

20 Tips for Good Behavior for the Adult Woman with ADHD

In this last part of the text, we will be looking at providing you with some final practical advice for the adult woman suffering from ADHD to have a good overall life.

These are tips that start from the beginning, then a summary of the advice given so far and in addition others that will improve many aspects of your life in general. Let's see together what are these 20 tips.

Self-Assessment and Diagnosis

One of the best pieces of advice we can give you, regarding ADHD, we have already given you: is, to try to get a diagnosis as soon as possible. You can make an initial self-evaluation if you believe, also thanks to the reading of these two manuals, that you have ADHD, even though you have not yet had an official diagnosis. In any case, try to make the ADHD diagnosis process even easier and more conscious. On the internet, you will be able to find many self-assessment tests that will make you feel, at least prepared, towards a positive diagnosis of this pathology.

Feel relieved after a definite diagnosis
One very helpful piece of advice would be to not lose heart if your ADHD diagnosis comes back positive. Think about it: the fact that you have had ADHD all your life could have a very positive effect on your self-perception, providing a very plausible justification for some of your behaviors and failures. One study, in this regard, revealed that women who had just been diagnosed with ADHD were much more likely to forgive themselves for past mistakes. Beyond that, many of them, perceive the feeling that they can have more control of their current lives. In addition, the knowledge that you do not have some mental disorder without a specific name or cause could give you a huge feeling of relief. Which you will certainly need.

Check coexisting conditions **and comorbidities**
Comorbidities with ADHD were listed to you in the previous manual. Here we remind you that this type of disorder rarely "travels" on its own, which means that you may experience one or more co-occurring conditions with your ADHD. However, this should not generate alarm or panic in you. Knowing what conditions you have allows you to treat each one directly, which in turn means you can be the healthiest. The most common co-occurring condition that women with ADHD may experience in comorbidity is depression, anxiety, alcoholism, eating disorders, and chronic insomnia. Sometimes it can be really difficult to figure out which co-occurring condition may arise with ADHD, as they can mask each other; therefore, it is most important that you work closely with your doctor to get a clearer picture of these co-occurring conditions.

Don't feel perpetually guilty about the clutter
A good tip for you is to let go of your "household" guilt. Basically, we tell you that it is useless to always feel guilty or ashamed of the fact that, often your home is not tidy, such as that of your neighbors or acquaintances. Unfortunately, and it is right to accept it, you definitely have more difficulties than them in tidying up and organizing your home. There are more important things in life to

worry about. At the very most, through some of the interventions we have outlined in the specific treatment section, you learn different ways to organize and clean your home. If you just can't, and of course you have the ability, ask for help by hiring a cleaner. Or you can simply have your spouse or other family members help you with the things you are not particularly good at, while you can focus on something more comfortable for you. Guilt free!

Some tips on driving with ADHD

When it comes to driving, for women with ADHD, especially with the inattentive subtype, it could pose a greater risk of accidents while driving. To remedy this problem, there are a few steps that could prove to be very helpful. First of all, consider driving a car with a manual transmission rather than an automatic one. This is because having to change gears often forces you to be more engaged and focused in your driving. Before you start driving, then, it is important that you remove all possible sources of distraction. In this regard, turning off your phone is important so that you cannot be distracted by incoming calls or messages. Also speaking of calls: never talk on the phone, even with an earpiece. Also, whether you have ADHD or not, it is always important not to drink or take drugs, as they can further reduce attention. Also, avoid medications that create drowsiness.

Let go of perfectionism

Let go of the need to be perfect. With ADHD, being perfect turns out to be a utopia. Then you must always assume that perfection, does not exist. Not for anyone! While striving for perfection may help you feel that you have more control over your life, it can be detrimental, especially when it comes to time management: you may find yourself spending too much time on small things that don't have a big impact on your life at the expense of more important things. For example, you might spend hours and hours finding the perfect font size for a possible business report, while neglecting to start a presentation that's due tomorrow. Or trying to prepare the perfect dish while neglecting other more pressing family tasks. From the moment you raise the bar for yourself, the constant internal pressure to do everything perfectly can also lead you to give up on a task (even not start it at all) because it is overwhelming and too much work for you. Instead of continuing to torture yourself with pressure on yourself to meet incredibly high standards that are unattainable in practice, work on yourself to put things in perspective. And try to be your best without having to be compulsorily "perfect".

Don't despair if you spend more time on some activities

If there's one thing that many women with ADHD often complain about, it's the fact that they definitely take longer to do things that other people do in less time. And that speed is not one's strong suit. To give some practical examples, there are regular tasks that need to be done in the workplace, perhaps a response to emails, filing forms or spreadsheets, etc., and you will often notice that your colleagues are faster than you. If this is true for you, then what you may not realize is that you should not despair about this but you should start developing an awareness that there are some things that people do faster. But that does not mean that there are no activities that you can do just as fast. It's not about competing, but noting down the tasks that you can be faster and more efficient at can help you not only increase your self-esteem but also increase your skills, both in the home and in the workplace.

How to manage the Hyperactivity Factor

If you are an ADHD adult female with prevalent hyperactivity symptoms, find a way to give vent to your perpetually active self. Whether it's a specific exercise or hobby, or sport, carve out time each day to vent this component as much as possible. The best advice we can give you is to exercise, in the morning if possible. It will then help you feel focused and calm for the rest of the day. You can also use, sports activities, in many positive ways. To meet new people and socialize, or find people who appreciate this hyperactive side of you.

Form or join a women's ADHD support group

As we previously explained when we talked about alternative interventions for ADHD in the adult woman, we already recommended that you seek out a support group. Often the struggle with ADHD in women is greater than you may realize. Breaking out of a mold of impossible expectations related to the many roles a woman is called upon to fulfill is easier with the support of others. Or other women like you, specifically. It especially helps to keep you from feeling alone. In fact, many women find support groups for women with ADHD to be a powerful source of encouragement and understanding. In this greater climate of understanding, women with ADHD can work harder to develop more realistic expectations of themselves and to develop better strategies for dealing with situations that, because of ADHD, still seem impossible.

Raise awareness of ADHD and its effects on you among those around you

We have already reiterated this in the first manual. Your partners, especially when they are still unaware of your ADHD disorder, may feel anger and resentment toward a poorly maintained home or misbehaving children. Unknowingly, they associate this with the fact that their spouse or partner "just doesn't care." Even if you know about the disorder, your partner is still not always understanding. On the other hand, as for the parents of the woman with ADHD, they too may react rather judgmental, wondering why their daughter's home is always so messy and why she may need more emotional, physical or financial help than, say, her non-ADHD siblings. Non-ADHD friends may, intentionally or unintentionally, give negative messages or little understanding toward you. For all of these reasons, it is really critical for you to work to educate all "others close to you" about your life and the impact of ADHD on it. This will serve you but also your loved ones. By doing so, in fact, you will be able to make sure that they can support you and help you solve problems instead of judging and blaming you. It's hard enough to be a woman with ADHD, with all the disabling situations involved, so you won't need to be surrounded by family and friends who blame you for your difficulties. You are, in fact, entitled to all the support you can get.

Invite the partner to participate in a support group

To give yourself more support in struggling with ADHD symptoms, it would be very helpful if you invited your partner to join a local adult ADHD support group. It is often a boon to hear from other people with ADHD, especially when they describe their challenges and marriages that are often challenged by this condition. Your partner may be more open to change when he or she hears that other husbands are dealing with the same situation. In addition, testimonials may prove helpful in following up on strategies others have learned to live a more peaceful and better managed life with their spouse with ADHD.

Create an ADHD-friendly environment at home

You work daily to create an "ADHD-friendly" dysfunctional behavior-proof environment within your home. However, this environment is not just about you. Chances are, if you have been diagnosed with ADHD, one or more of your children probably have it as well. If you can succeed in creating an understanding environment in which other family members can feel comfortable, accepting and good-humored, the frequency of emotional outbursts will decrease and you will be better able to save more energy for the positive side of things. Building an ADHD-friendly home environment also results in improved overall relationships within the family. But, on top of all that it allows you to develop home routines that will serve to keep you from feeling burnt out, exhausted and overwhelmed. Not less, the pro-ADHD home environment, concretely allows you to identify the causes of chronic stress and work to reduce them, as well as to reduce the most disabling issues of this disorder. Basically, it's about becoming a problem-solving family instead of blaming and blaming. Also learn to assign, again within the home tasks based on strengths and preferences.

And if you just can't create an ADHD-friendly environment, consider working with an ADHD coach or professional organizer for help in creating and implementing your ideal ADHD-friendly home environment.

Create spaces of refuge and calm within your home environment

In addition to being able to organize an environment of positivity towards ADHD, it would be equally important to create escape spaces, or rather a refuge or "calming spaces" for family members who are prone to emotional outbursts when they feel stressed. Not just for you, but for your children as well. A calming space can be any quiet area that provides a comfortable place to lie down and contains stress-relieving items, such as a device to play soft music, a soft blanket, and, for children, perhaps a stuffed toy.

Simplify your life as much as possible

Most women with ADHD are often overloaded with commitments and backlogs of work and very often are exhausted and overwhelmed. If this is the case for you, look for ways to reduce your schedule and make your life as easy as possible. This applies to your children as well. Don't be afraid to deprive your child of certain commitments by trying unnecessarily to keep up with other children's schedules and commitments. Make life easier for them, too.

Aerobic activity: a possible lifeline

Even if you think that time is already a challenge for you and you are constantly struggling with it, the most important thing you can do to improve brain function (and reduce your struggles with ADHD) is just aerobic exercise. It's not about compulsory gym memberships or spending money on expensive classes, we are aware that this is something that is really hard for you to handle. But it is possible to do good aerobic exercise, easily at home. In fact, we recommend that you find half an hour a day to exercise at home, perhaps by creating a routine. A routine that helps you make sure that exercise happens at a specific time that you can't make excuses for. A routine is created in at least one week. Try to be consistent, maybe every morning as soon as you get up. It will help you focus better, feel energetic and positive about facing the day, and also help you sleep better.

Remove friends and acquaintances who criticize you and don't understand the situation

To create more congenial situations for your problems with ADHD, in addition to, as we suggested above, creating an environment of people in your family who understand and support you, you will need to try to have friends and acquaintances who appreciate the best in you, despite the condition. More importantly, don't be surrounded by people who judge you for your flaws or the problems you have with ADHD. Try to avoid putting yourself among people who will stir up feelings of inadequacy in you because of their perfectionist expectations and negative comparisons. For this reason, one of the best pieces of advice we can offer you is to steer away from uncomfortable situations and negativity...people included!

Take breaks every day

Taking breaks throughout the day is essential for you, especially to reduce stress. In fact, try to recognize feelings of overwhelm before you are completely exhausted, and perhaps pass your exhaustion on to your family members, and children in particular. Look for ways to take a break, recharge and get back to being calmer and more peaceful. But these moments of respite are not just about the possible mother with ADHD. This advice also applies if you are a single woman trying to carry on with ADHD, facing increasingly difficult daily challenges. It may be necessary in your case to avoid spending too many hours at the office and neglecting self-care by giving yourself a break. Many single-career women with ADHD work hard to manage ADHD patterns at work but completely neglect their family or relationship life. In general, therefore all women with ADHD, need to consciously find time to "do nothing," to relax and rejuvenate.

Learn to delegate

Women with ADHD need to learn to discard all excess activities that could bring them additional stress. The easiest way would be to delegate various activities in their daily lives to create more balance. Organizational tasks in life are more challenging, in fact if you are a woman with ADHD. You could, for example, invest in household help, or a nanny to help you care for the children. Either way, looking for ways to delegate your tasks may be one of the best investments you could make in developing a more ADHD-friendly lifestyle. Definitely a lifestyle that is less stressful and doesn't lead you to further exacerbate your ADHD.

Take specialized courses for parents with children with ADHD.

A typical situation we have often pointed to is a family with a woman with ADHD who often finds herself also being the parent of a child with ADHD. From this perspective they face an even greater challenge. Even more so if they are single parents, the challenge could be really debilitating and further promote ADHD. Basically a situation that could prove to be completely unmanageable. On the outside looking in, it can be easy for other parents to judge a woman with ADHD when her children misbehave. But what every parent of a child with ADHD knows is that children with ADHD do not act and behave totally differently from others. In a way that is, precisely, dysfunctional. Children with ADHD, we know by now, are more challenging, need more commitment and support, and often have special educational and psychological needs. If you have a child with ADHD, it is important that you seek this support through training. A specialized course on the needs of the child with ADHD and how to work to help them could be lifesaving for both you and your child. CHADD, (the national organization that supports families with ADHD), in this regard, provides "parent-to-parent" training groups that are highly convenient and can prove extremely valuable, not only providing you with the proper parenting tools but also the support and encouragement of other parents who truly understand the parenting challenges you face every day. As the mother of a child with ADHD, you have a rather daunting and demanding job. So don't blame yourself or allow others to judge you. Instead, focus on getting the training and support you need.

Learn to focus on your best self

Sometimes, you are so overwhelmed by the daily challenges you face due to ADHD that you never allow yourself to be focused on your talents, your strengths, and the things you love most. Basically on the best of yourself. As a woman with ADHD, your main goal should be to understand and accept yourself. As we have been saying since the beginning of the first manual. Accept yourself, just as you are. Therefore, try not to measure your success through someone else's yardstick and comparison. Instead, always reward your daily progress as a woman with ADHD, and always work to create opportunities to be yourself and give your best. By doing so, you will be able to concretely bring out the best in yourself.

These 20 tips conclude the penultimate chapter of the text. In the next and final chapter, you will have a comprehensive guide on how to manage a very critical factor for a woman with ADHD, namely time.

Chapter 17: Mini-guide on how to manage time effectively

How does ADHD affect poor time management?

We have reiterated many times that the presence of ADHD in adults makes time management difficult. According to Prof. Russell Barkley, time management is: "a disability, almost invisible, that afflicts those with ADHD." This is true, even more so, for the adult woman with this type of disorder. But why does this happen?

Because, typically, a brain with ADHD is inherently unable to anticipate and plan for the future. This lack of planning typically manifests itself in two ways:

1. People with ADHD often have a "very short time horizon ". This simply means that a person with ADHD has a time "*horizon*" in which it is difficult to feel motivated to act, at least in the long run.
2. Another way in which ADHD interferes with the ability to plan for the future is through "temporal discounting". This is a term used in economics that reflects, a particular truth: the further into the future a reward or punishment is, the less attention we want to pay to it in the present moment. Therefore, there will be less tendency to want to plan and manage a possible long term. This is true for everyone - not just people with ADHD - feeling the present more strongly, because it is harder to do challenging things right away by not having immediate positive feedback. However, people with ADHD tend to always choose the option with the most immediate payoff, as their impulsive component wants "everything and now." From the perspective of a person with ADHD disorder, therefore, close gratification becomes more important than punishment, or a negative effect that may come later.

Because of these two modes, people with ADHD, especially women, will obsessively seek to have a long-term advantage by often going through stressful situations, disappointments, and failures. And for these reasons, they will have poor time management.

Understanding the difficulties of time management with ADHD

Before we provide you with a final mini-guide with which to get clear on time management with ADHD, we want to clarify a concept for you. This concept is about time management and its difficulties. Time management difficulty, in fact, is a fairly common factor for adult women with ADHD. To understand this type of difficulty, it is necessary to do a little analysis of all the possible factors that prevent you from properly managing your time: you may, in fact, because of ADHD completely lose track of time. These difficulties in time management could lead you to have just as much difficulty in following certain plans or underestimate how much time you need to spend on different activities. You may also find that you spend too much time on a single activity, which is known as hyperfocus. Because of this hyperfocus, you may find that you are unable to do anything else.

All of these time management difficulties, can often leave you feeling overwhelmed, frustrated and, no less, exhausted. To remedy these problems and, understand the importance of your time management difficulties, below are some very useful tips to help you manage your time better.

Best tips for time management

Here we are at the actual mini-guide, where you will be listed all the best tips for optimal time management for a woman with ADHD:

Never plan too far in advance

Planning too far in advance for adult women with ADHD may prove to be unnecessary, if not entirely counterproductive. As with many other skills, time management is different for each individual person, and even more complicated for people with ADHD. Good time management boils down to this: "effectively using the present moment to create a better future." Based on this adage, you will therefore have no need to plan your time very far in advance, because you will only risk seeing all your plans go up in smoke. In fact, most goals and projects in life require consistent effort over time, in exchange for long-term positive impact. But all of this is quite complicated for a person with ADHD, so planning ahead is almost always impossible. Rather, it would be best to bring into play all the external tools, treatments, and motivational strategies for better time management by the adult woman with ADHD.

Alternative solutions to avoid the all and now

As we explained in the first paragraph, the most deleterious pattern for a person with ADHD is poor time management due to the "all and soon" logic. How can people with ADHD counteract this today/now focused mindset? Through different strategies. One of these is related to the externalization of time. In other words, when the "internal" clock of a person with ADHD is rather unreliable, and one often loses track of time, one must rely more on external clocks. One can then rely on the fact:

- Wear watches
- Use timers that show the time remaining
- Set alarm clocks/alarms to remind you of deadlines/commitments
- Schedule things to do directly into a weekly, or monthly, calendar with specific times and schedules.

Maximize motivation

Time for a person with ADHD is often linked to a lack of motivation. A striking example is that of a possible distant horizon, which for a person with impulsive traits typical of ADHD, is impossible to accept. To exploit (and maintain) motivation before it is too late, it is important to "visualize" well the time available.

In order for this visualization to be effective, we must first recognize the use of common lies/justifications that we tell ourselves, or others, to justify poor time management. It is essential to try to avoid these justifications as much as possible so that we can develop better long-term time management. And increase motivation.

Eliminate distractions as much as possible

We know by now that, a hallmark symptom of ADHD is inattention, so it is easy to get caught up in distraction, which in turn can cause even the most effective time management strategies to be ignored. Since it is very easy for you to be distracted, it will be important to set up your work environment, or desk to eliminate distractions and manage the temptation to abandon the task at hand. This means that you can implement some of the most commonly used techniques to eliminate distractions, especially in the workplace. These techniques include:
- Block tempting Web sites on your computer.
- Set your phone to "silent" mode or turn it off until you finish your work.
- Face the desk toward the wall so you are not tempted to look out the window.

Avoid continual procrastination

A typical characteristic of people with ADHD, especially adults, is precisely that of procrastination. Adult women with ADHD, in particular, tend to put off long-term goals/tasks because they imagine the effort to be much greater, more complicated, and more difficult than it actually is in reality. But waiting until the last minute because the project seems too difficult - or avoiding it altogether because it involves too much risk - tends to become a constant and a huge cloud of negativity, because the longer you procrastinate or avoid something, the more difficult (or unlikely) the project or goal becomes to accomplish. So the solution would be to, however, set daily mini-goals that are achievable in the shortest possible time.

Try to keep the most negative feelings under control at all times

Even when it comes to time management, often, women with ADHD put off the task because they feel uncomfortable doing it, without knowing exactly why. In some cases, the project might simply seem boring, so apathy and lack of motivation take over. Other women, on the other hand, might experience excessive worry regarding possible failure - causing them to procrastinate as a way to postpone the anxiety they feel. Apathy and anxiety require different solutions, and it is impossible to know which solution to try until you identify the root cause of your procrastination. One way, then, might be to try to keep the more negative feelings at bay perhaps by getting help through therapy and support groups.

Finally...some super practical daily tips

Here are some final super practical tips that will help you daily with time factor management:

1. Get as organized as you can, whether you have to go to work, run errands or tackle household chores, it can be helpful to write down and highlight your top priorities. You may find it helpful to create a schedule the night before you go to bed (so not too far in advance) so that you can start your day off right. Having a "plan of attack" will help you feel calmer throughout the day, making you achieve fewer goals and, increase your motivation at the same time.
2. Identify your strengths and weaknesses. Many women with ADHD complain, as we know, that they take longer to accomplish tasks than other people. One way to remedy this problem on a day-to-day basis is to start recognizing what you can do faster and what takes longer. When you have a clear and balanced picture of your strengths and weaknesses, your motivation and self-esteem will especially benefit you.
3. Allow yourself more time throughout the day. Make sure you have plenty of time to finish a daily project by perhaps allowing yourself a little extra 10-minute break every 30 minutes. They will help avoid boredom and distraction and complete a task.
4. Also, assign yourself time limits. By assigning yourself a limited amount of time for each task (perhaps through the use of the previously mentioned timer) you will have a warning when the time is up. The timer gives you an audible signal to stop what you are working on so that you do not lose track of time and challenge yourself to complete the task.

These were the best recommendations for optimal time management, despite the presence of ADHD. Finally, in the next final section, we will examine a model designed specifically for time management in association with ADHD.

The Grossman Model

The Grossman Model is a series of strategies designed to improve time management.
According to Grossman, the best prescription, specifically, for being on time and managing time better, includes:
- Plan ahead (not too far). This planning, in fact, happens, daily.
- Employing strategies that utilize individual preferences and personal style.
- Using external signals to indicate elapsed time

Essentially, these are the strategies we outlined to you earlier. In this model, they are all incorporated in the form of a challenge. Let's take a look at what this is specifically about:

First challenge: planning many activities

What to do if you find yourself involved in too many activities? Grossman says that this over-scheduling happens quite often for women with ADHD. Unfortunately, over-commitment and over-scheduling simply lead us to frustration. And failure or surrender may be near. However, the scholar proposes solutions in the face of this type of challenge:
- ✓ One such solution would be to opt for a digital planner that takes into consideration size, technology, ease of use, portability, color, and sensitivity.
- ✓ Another solution might be to pin times for known, set, key events such as work schedules, meal times, carpools, and standing appointments.
- ✓ Create a to-do list and then no more than 3-5 high-priority items to complete in a given day. This is, in essence, a matter of prioritizing

Challenge 2: Have what you need to get out on time

It's time to get in the car and head to your next destination, but the necessary items are scattered around the house. You may be wondering where your glasses, keys, etc. have gone. now don't panic, but there may be possible solutions, according to Grossman.

Here are the possible solutions:
1. Establish places of proximity for when you go out. As a practical example, you might place, near the door, your keys, wallets, backpacks, and purses. Get in the habit of putting all those items you need in a place that is easy to remember every time you are about to leave the house.
2. Store items you need to take with you in the morning in the designated place or on the floor near the door. Encourage all family members to do the same so that you can make your life easier.

Challenge 3: Avoid not knowing what to wear or bring with you in the morning

Preparing clothes to wear the night before would be the ideal solution to avoid panicking the next day, perhaps finding yourself with nothing to wear. A woman with ADHD should avoid having to decide what to wear at the last minute. Or perhaps finding yourself having to sort through office supplies or school supplies for your children.

Here are the possible solutions proposed, in this case by Grossman:
1. Reduce morning stress by getting everything ready the night before. Gather all items for your morning outfit (even the kids'), including shoes and accessories, before going to bed.
2. Establish and post, perhaps in the kitchen a list of the morning routine. And establish the materials needed as well, perhaps getting help from other family members.

Challenge 4: Avoid losing track of time

How many times have you been so immersed in an activity, whether at the computer or at work and completely lost track of time?

This happens quite frequently to women with ADHD. Perhaps you find yourself super busy with an interesting activity, but you risk completely losing your sense of time and, as a result, missing (or being late for) an important meeting. Possible solutions, **according to Grossman and her model, to remedy such problems could be:**

1. Keep a timer strategically set to ring or vibrate as an exact external indication of elapsed time. You can also use a combination of a vibrating alarm on your watch set as a warning signal and an independent timer set 15 minutes later as a reminder to turn off your computer in a timely manner.
2. Set a cell phone to vibrate every 10 or 15 minutes. When the alarm goes off, use it as a cue to orient yourself in time. Then ask yourself, after the alarm is going off, if what you're doing is more important at this precise moment, and if you have other activities to do.

These were some of the challenges of the Grossman model and all the possible solutions. Our mini-guide concludes our second discussion. Following these tips will be very helpful in ensuring that you can manage, as optimally as possible, the time you have available. These, along with the various tips that have been provided to you throughout the other chapters, could be a real turning point for you and ensure that you can deal with your life as a woman with ADHD in the best possible way.

Conclusions

In this second, much more practical handbook, you are given a lot of guidance on how to manage ADHD.
After carefully reviewing the symptomatology, causes and diagnosis of the disease, we went over each downside and, how to make sure it can be contained.
From a comprehensive look at all possible therapies to practical tips that relate to daily life, you'll be able to manage ADHD in the best way possible.
This of course by associating it with a treatment that is targeted to your needs, your symptoms, and especially the discomfort that this disease creates for you on a daily basis.
With these two guides, we sincerely hope that we can help you as much as possible in your struggle with a disorder, sometimes as disabling, as ADHD.

Manufactured by Amazon.ca
Acheson, AB